IF YOU DIDN'T BRING JERKY, WHAT DID I JUST EAT?

*A note on the title: I made it up. It's just one of several titles I came up with one night. Among others that were rejected: 1) *Don't Shoot Until That Deer Finishes Mowing My Lawn;* 2) *Giant Bucks I Have Missed;* and 3) *Fifty Ways to Leave Your Tree Stand.* In the end, we went with the one in big letters on the opposite page. — B.H.

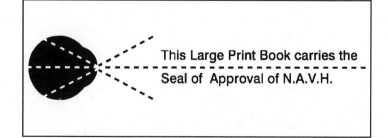

This Large Print Book carries the Seal of Approval of N.A.V.H.

IF YOU DIDN'T BRING JERKY, WHAT DID I JUST EAT?*

MISADVENTURES IN HUNTING, FISHING, AND THE WILDS OF SUBURBIA

BILL HEAVEY

THORNDIKE PRESS

A part of Gale, Cengage Learning

GALE
CENGAGE Learning

Detroit • New York • San Francisco • New Haven, Conn • Waterville, Maine • London

LIBRARY OF CONGRESS CATALOGING-IN-PUBLICATION DATA

Heavey, Bill.
    If you didn't bring jerky, what did I just eat? : misadventures in hunting, fishing, and the wilds of suburbia / by Bill Heavey.
        p. cm.
    ISBN-13: 978-1-4104-0590-6 (hardcover : alk. paper)
    ISBN-10: 1-4104-0590-7 (hardcover : alk. paper)
    1. Hunting stories, American. 2. Fishing stories, American.
3. Heavey, Bill. 4. Large type books. I. Title.
SK33.H44 2007
799.29—dc22   2007051709

Published in 2008 by arrangement with Grove/Atlantic, Inc.

For William F. Heavey Jr., 1920–2007

Whose poet spirit lived
the warrior code:
cheerful always,
always bold

*A man knows when he is growing old
because he begins to look like his father.*
— Gabriel García Márquez

CONTENTS

FOREWORD

Field & Stream magazine has been around for more than a hundred years, and in all that time, there have been only three men who were talented enough to write humor for it on a regular basis.

Ed Zern was a genius who dealt in a kind of wry, detached zaniness that people found irresistible. His "Exit Laughing" column, which ran on the magazine's back page from 1958 until 1994, could have appeared in *The New Yorker* just as easily as in *Field & Stream.*

Patrick F. McManus, who now writes the back-page column for *Outdoor Life,* would rather get a belly laugh than a chuckle. He is the man to see for broad humor. The world he created featured himself as a blundering preteen kid and a regular cast of characters with names such as Rancid Crabtree and Retch Sweeney. It was a spiritual throwback to the 1950s sitcoms where

11

people laughed and no one really got hurt.

Bill Heavey taps into a third type of comedy. It is the variety in which you can see yourself and laugh, or wince, or even cry. Bill is an everyman who may be the most inept sportsman ever to grace the magazine's pages. On the other hand, he may simply be the most honest. He mines the very failures we all encounter but that most of us take pains to conceal. In short, his boneheaded mistakes are our bone-headed mistakes. When applied to hunting and fishing, which are largely based on competence, dexterity, and skill, these mistakes are amplified, and the consequences are often severe. If, for example, Bill tells you that he spilled scalding coffee in his crotch while driving to his tree stand before first light, you can bet he has the burns to prove it and will show them to you given half a chance.

This idea — that enthusiasm trumps skill — is something of a revolutionary concept in outdoor magazines. Before Heavey, outdoor writers were sunburned Eagle Scout types who were seemingly born with rod and gun in hand and were always successful at their pursuits. They could survive for weeks with nothing but some matches and a box of fishing hooks. Heavey, on the other hand, came to hunting in his late thirties, largely as a way to expand what he could write about. He is neither sunburned nor an Eagle Scout, but he does have the maniacal zeal of the late convert. In recent years he has become obsessed with whitetail deer, which have consistently proven themselves higher on the evolutionary scale than he is.

Unlike say, Ted Trueblood, the famous *Field & Stream* writer who spent his days in the glorious mountains of southwestern Idaho, Heavey lives in the suburbs of Washington, D.C. He hunts for shed deer antlers in strips of woods loud with the hum of the Beltway, and he fishes for largemouth bass in the Potomac as police boats comb the water for terrorists. It is not a romantic outdoor life, at least not in the conventional sense. Bill works his hunting and fishing schedule around the duties of a modern dad: mowing the lawn; paying the bills; and ferrying his daughter Emma to school, the dentist, play dates, and toy stores. At the same time, he tries to introduce her to the world he loves: learning to stalk by sneaking up on a neighbor's mechanical Christmas reindeer, fishing a suburban lake for bluegills, and imitating the calls of doves in the backyard. In other words, he lives like most of us, and perhaps that is why his pieces are so resonant. For him, being at large in the woods for even a few hours is a spiritual journey, and the fact that the enterprise is doomed to failure more often than not is almost incidental. While he may not be in the accelerated class, skills-wise, Heavey has the heart of a true hunter. He knows that the animal is a necessary actor, but that the experience of hunting is the real trophy.

For the past several years, Bill and I have carried on a war of words in the pages of *Field & Stream,* never missing a chance to exchange insults. But since I am saying nice things (or what I think are nice things) about Heavey, and since this will never happen again, I should point out that he has also written some of the most heart-wrenching stories I've ever read. I don't know of any writer who can hit from both sides of the plate as well as he. One reader wrote in suggesting a Kleenex warning appear next to any of his stories in which the transition from humor to pathos is especially quick. But this would be like warning the audience when the Road Runner is about to lead Wile E. Coyote under a boulder that will fall on his head. It would ruin all the fun.

Invariably, when I introduce myself as an

editor of *Field & Stream,* people do not ask about what I do or how I came to be at the magazine. They ask what Heavey is really like. The answer: He is an extremely well read and intelligent individual who marches not just to the beat of a different drummer, but to the beat of a whole different drum and bugle corps. I find him entertaining to talk to but am leery of being around him because he tends to attract misfortune. Spending time outdoors (or indoors, for that matter) with Heavey is like standing in an open field in a thunderstorm with a graphite rod in your hand. It's not a question of whether the lightning is going to strike but when.

In closing, I urge you to buy this book. If you have it handy you can pick it up and have a laugh anytime you want. It can also be used as a doorstop, or as emergency fire-starting material. For no other reason, buy it to support an endangered species, a writer who sees himself and the world he lives in for what they are and can still manage to smile. In short, Bill needs the money. He certainly can't feed himself on what he brings home from the woods.

— David E. Petzal

INTRODUCTION

In my defense, I am not responsible for the half-truths, exaggerations, and outright lies in this book of fishing and hunting tales. I blame my parents, who routinely packed me off to summer camp starting at the age of 10 simply because I had begun to dismantle the house with a Phillips head screwdriver. It was at these rural juvenile holding facilities, first in New Hampshire, then in North Carolina, that I discovered the pleasures of watching a red-and-white bobber. I've lost count of the hours I spent daydreaming about the huge fish with my name on its side that would cause the bobber to vanish.

In time, the other boys took pity on me, informing me that the bobber was only truly effective when cast into the water above a baited hook. (I had been staring at it and my fishing rod as they rested in the bunkhouse rafter above my bed.) At this point things got really interesting. I discovered that I loved fishing in water even more than fishing in air. The idea that a boy as inept and awkward as me could be transformed into a hero at any moment had immense appeal. It never happened, of course. But the habit of failure got into my blood, and I kept at it.

One day many years later, I sent off a story I had written about fishing for smallmouths in the rivers around my stomping grounds in Maryland and Virginia to the offices of *Field & Stream* magazine in New York. It was not long before a series of misunderstandings led to my fabrications regularly appearing in print.

Emboldened by success, I decided at the tender age of 35 to try hunting. This, I reasoned, would give me material to lie about during the months when it was too cold to lie about fishing. To my surprise — and to the horror of my parents, who happily ate beef, chicken, fish, pork, squab, lamb, and veal but thought it was reprehensible that anyone would actually kill an innocent animal — I discovered in hunting the same obsessive-compulsive satisfactions that I had found in fishing.

The world of outdoor writing is populated by distressingly competent people who can match the hatch, recognize a staging area, and predict where a bass or a buck will be found as easily as I hook a bush on a back cast. But hunting and fishing are far too important to be left to the capable alone. This is a book for the rest of us: those with more enthusiasm than competence. The best memories cannot be preserved by taxidermy. If you have ever pulled your lure out of the mouth of a big fish as it was about to chomp down, missed a deer at 14 yards, or had a turkey peer curiously around the wrong side of the tree you were sitting against to see how you produced the sound of a crow choking on a fish bone, you are in the right place. I count you as a brother and true outdoorsman.

In closing, I throw myself upon the mercy of the court and ask that if I am to be incarcerated, I be allowed access to a red-and-white bobber. Even if it's unattached to a hook and line.

■ ■ ■ ■

I
STALKING IN SLIPPERS:
THE NOVICE YEARS

■ ■ ■ ■

THE DISTANCE
TO TROUBLE

Maybe taking my new laser rangefinder to my nephew's wedding wasn't the best idea I ever had, but bow season was coming up fast. As all bowhunters know, those long summer hours on the practice range mean zip when the moment comes and the deer you sighted at 32 yards turns out to have been standing just 17 yards from your tree. Frankly, judging distances is an area in which Stevie Wonder and I are about equally skilled. Oh, I know the basic "tricks of the trade": If you look through your peep and see individual hairs, the deer is quite close. If you can see the whole deer and a fair amount of the real estate surrounding it, the deer is not close.

Other than that, I'm lost. I figured I needed advanced help, the kind that only $350 buys you. By the time I ordered the laser rangefinder, I had convinced myself that it was as necessary to my continued survival as oxygen, water, or Fletch-Tite.

It did not disappoint. Arriving the morning we were due to fly to Indianapolis for the wedding, the Bushnell Yardage Pro Compact 600 lay seductively wrapped in tissue paper and a black neoprene carrying case. I picked it up and started fiddling. It had simultaneous multiple target acquisition capability like an AWACS plane; reflective, rain, and zip-thru laser modes for all-weather capability; an LCD gauge showing distances up to 600 yards with plus-or-minus 1-yard accuracy; and a 4X perma-focus sighting system with a tiny box in the middle of the crosshairs that looked like something off a smart bomb. I was smitten. I stashed it in my carry-on.

The lady at the X-ray machine was suspicious. "Why you got a camera with three eyes on it?" she asked. I explained that you look through one lens, while the others send out a laser beam, which — But at the words "laser beam," she cut me off as if I'd said "pipe bomb." She immediately waved over a large gentleman wearing an even larger security blazer. "Tony," she called loudly, pointing at me.

Tony ran his wand over me to see if I'd managed to arm myself in the 15 seconds since passing through the metal detector. Then he wiped my new toy with a pad that detects explosives residue. Then he held the rangefinder up to his own eye. "See, you push that button, and it tells you how far away stuff is," I explained nervously. I was afraid that maybe rangefinders fit into some new category of things you couldn't bring into airports. Tony aimed it down the long corridor and hit the button. "Hey," he said. "It's 78 yards to the men's room sign. Cool." He smiled and handed it back to me.

Whoever was driving the bride to the church got lost. We sat in a stifling hot Methodist Quonset hut with zero ventilation, three crying babies, and pews built to remind the sitter that earthly existence is not meant to be fun. Numb with boredom and sweating heavily, I slipped the rangefinder out of my pocket and focused on the organist. I would have bet he was a good 30 yards off, but the LCD read 19. My arrow would have whizzed 2 feet over his head and stuck in the big pipe behind him. Someone tapped me on the shoulder. It was my wife's sister's mother-in-law. "Would you mind taking a picture of little Ashley and me?" she smiled.

"Happy to," I said. I aimed and pushed the button.

"My, that camera's quiet."

"New model," I explained.

The jig was finally up at the reception. I was once again overestimating distances — the buffet table that I guessed at 41 yards was a mere 27 — when one of my younger cousins came up behind me. "That thing isn't a camera," Luke, 14, said triumphantly. I felt if anybody could appreciate my new toy, it would be a kid, so I took him into my confidence and showed him how it worked.

He began sending infrared beams all over the room. Then suddenly he burst out laughing. "Check it out, dude. Aunt Laura's waist is 46 yards away, but her butt's only 45 yards!"

"Gimme that thing back. And don't you tell anybody about it, or I'll break your fingers. Now beat it." Last I saw him, he was 24 yards out and headed toward Aunt Laura. I made a beeline for the door.

THE ACCESS CONSULTANT

The lady of the farm — with a chain saw, sun hat, and a look on her face like she hasn't had a good laugh since the Johnstown Flood — makes me 20 yards out as I pull into the farm's rutted drive. She yanks the chain saw into being and walks away. Almost as an afterthought, she sticks her free hand in the air and twirls one finger in a circle. It's a miracle of nonverbal communication, that twirling finger. It says, *Don't even think about asking to hunt deer here. Just turn your car around and git.* I do.

The next place has a gravel road lined with honey locust trees and woods on either side. Even from my car, I can see deer trails everywhere. Around back is a man sitting in the shade with a glass of beer and the sports section. I introduce myself awkwardly and ask if he has a problem with deer eating his plants. "Eat the hell outta my wife's garden," he says cheerfully.

I move to Stage Two, telling him that maybe we can help each other. He raises a hand just as I'm getting to the part about how responsible I am. "At least you asked. I'll give you that. But last year, some bowhunter took out a horse we've had for 16 years. Broke my wife's heart. You seem like a nice enough feller, but I can't let you hunt here."

At the last try of the day, I trudge unhopefully to knock on the door of what looks like an empty house. Only it isn't empty. In fact, there's a woman standing stone still in the dimness of the screen porch. "Ma'am?" I say. "My name's Bill Hea —"

"I don't care if your name's Pat Sajak. Nobody hunts here."

I smile. I pivot. I leave.

Two weeks later, I'm at it again. Only this time I have a secret weapon — my father. My dad is 80. He doesn't hunt, doesn't fish, doesn't even approve of people who do. But he's as extroverted as they come.

When I pick him up, he's wearing a coat and tie and pants. When I mention that he might be a tad overdressed to talk to farmers, he says, "Always look your best for a sales call."

"This is a sales call?" I ask.

He stops and looks at me funny. "What

28

the heck d'you think it is?"

No one is home at the first place. No one seems to be at home at the second. The two of us stand on the front porch after knocking and listen for signs of life. "I'll check around back," he says. Two minutes later, I hear laughter coming from the other side of the house. On the flagstones out behind the back door, I see my father holding a glass of iced tea and talking to a couple about my age, who are so entranced they barely notice me. My father is already well into the story about how he accidentally burned down the refectory of the Church of the Redeemer on North Charles Street in Baltimore at a high school dance in the late 1930s.

The couple laugh and for the first time turn to have a look at me. "Oh, that's my son," my dad says offhandedly. "He'd like to bowhunt here if it's okay with you. He's a good boy." The two say sure, refill my father's glass, ask if he'd like a chair. And then he tells them the one about how the Rita Hayworth movie on the destroyer got mistaken for a German air attack.

"We'd just pulled into the harbor at Mers-el-Kebir in Algeria after a lot of combat in the North Atlantic," he says. "A supply ship had pulled up alongside and sent over Rita

Hayworth in the movie *Blood and Sand.* The harbor had been recently attacked and was completely blacked out, but the men were dying to see Rita Hayworth, so we rigged an overhead tarp up on deck and showed the movie under cover. Things were going fine until some knucklehead tossed a lit cigarette into the aluminum box where the film was stored. That thing went up like a torch, flames 20 feet in the air. And everybody in the harbor, thinking we were under attack, opened up with everything they had. After half an hour of fireworks, the harbormaster, thinking my ship had been hit, came over to assess the damage. I made the mistake of telling him exactly what happened, and he said, 'Mister, we just shot off five million bucks' worth of munitions so your men could watch Rita Hayworth. You get out of here, and don't come back.' "

As we're driving home, my father smiling at the thought of the new friends he's made, I'm thinking I could rent my father out to bowhunters as an "access consultant." I'd charge $300 an hour. I know guys who'd pay in a heartbeat.

SMELLS OF
THE SEASON

It is late November. Mom is off at a meeting and Molly, my 12-year-old stepdaughter, is late for her modern dance class. No problem, I tell her. I'll drive.

She plops down in the front seat, gags, and frantically unrolls the window. "Gross! Your car smells like the elephant house at the zoo!"

I'm a new and naive stepdad. I try the reasonable approach. Actually, I tell her, it's doe-in-estrus urine.

"Doe in extras?" she asks. "Like, there's more than one? And you spray their pee in your car?"

It's suddenly very important that this child not think I'm a mental patient in training. I launch into the simplified explanation of the rut. I tell her that when the girl deer are ready to be friends with the boy deer in the fall, their pee smells different than it does the rest of the year. This really excites the boy deer. And if you happen to be a hunter trying to lure the boy deer in, you can sometimes do this by putting a little doe-in-estrus on a rag tied to your feet when you walk to your stand.

She takes this all in and thinks it over for a few moments. Then she says, "That is so disgusting I can't even tell you." Her nose twitches again. "Are you carrying dirt in here?"

Uh-oh. She sniffs some more, then looks down at her feet and fishes up a little black disk from among the wrappers that once held Ring Dings, peanut-butter crackers, and toe warmers. I explain that it's the earth-scent wafer I put in the big Ziploc bag with my hunting clothes.

"How do they make a piece of plastic smell like dirt?"

I tell her I have no idea.

"So let me get this straight," she says finally. "You want where you've walked to smell like deer pee, but you want your clothes to smell like dirt."

"Yeah," I say at last. "That's basically it."

For a while, Molly is content to ride in silence. But my stepdaughter is blessed with a persistent curiosity. She turns and scans the backseat, plucking an unopened blister pack of red fox urine from the jumble.

"And this?" she demands.

"It's a cover scent. You spray a little of that on your shoes before you go in the woods."

"So dirt and doe pee aren't enough?" she probes. "You also want to smell like a fox has whizzed on your shoes?"

"Well, sorta," I mumble.

Molly has had enough. "Does Mommy know you do all this stuff?" she asks.

Mommy knows, I tell her. I'm praying she doesn't turn around again. There are scrape drippers back there. And Wrap-A-Rubs, scent neutralizers, and a busted bag of white buck-wallow powder on the floor.

Just as we are pulling up to the parking lot, she does turn around again. Guided by some invisible laser ray of curiosity, she heads right for pay dirt, the deer hunter's neutron bomb. Molly holds up two little tufts of nearly black deer hair encased within three layers of Ziploc bags. For a moment it looks as if she's about to open them and take a good whiff.

"Good gosh, child! Don't!" I blurt out. Inside the bags are two fresh tarsal glands from a 9-pointer a friend killed recently. One hit off those babies would knock Molly into the middle of next week.

"Jeez," she says. "I wasn't gonna hurt 'em."

"Those are tarsal glands," I tell her.

"So?" she asks.

"You better go, kiddo. We'll talk about those next time."

Molly sighs. "They're just another kind of pee, aren't they?" she says. It's not really a question. She already knows the answer. "At least I know what to get you for Christmas," she says.

"What?"

"Soap. A lot of it."

DEATH BY
MULTITOOL

If you've been on an airplane recently,[*]
you've noticed the following phenomenon:
The moment the announcement starts that
it's okay to use portable electronic devices,
nearly every person over the age of 8 simul-
taneously opens a laptop computer and
disappears into it. Me, I reach for my new
portable amusement park, my multitool.

Mine is a 21-function Schrade Tough
Tool, designed for a lifetime of faithful
service. The warranty says you're not supposed to throw it, use the blade as a screwdriver, or try to hammer things with it.
Other than that, you're pretty much on your
own. I open and close it about 50 times,
watching it do multitool jumping jacks and
transform itself from a small hunk of stain-

*Note that this piece was written before 9/11, when
you could carry anything short of a rocket launcher
aboard a plane.

less steel into an instrument of awesome capability. This alone is pretty entertaining. My only regret is that at the moment I have no cans to open, wires to strip, or anything in immediate need of sawing, scraping, filing, measuring, scribing, or disgorging. A multitool fairly radiates purpose, and it seems a shame not to be able to help it realize its full potential. I do use the Phillips head to tighten a loose screw in the Airfone in the seat back in front of me, prompting the guy ahead to turn around and glare.

With nothing mechanical in need of fixing, I turn to my personal appearance. Very discreetly, I shield my face with the airline magazine and go after a stray nose hair with the needle-nose pliers. At the exact moment I'm about to pull, the flight attendant's quizzical face appears about a foot above me. This startles me so much that I yank much harder than I meant to on the tool, which by this time is attached to much more real estate than I had planned. I basically clear-cut an entire forest of nasal hairs at once, which causes tears to well up in my eyes in great abundance. Flight attendants witness so many strange things that it's hard to know where the sight of a man with an 8-inch multitool halfway up his nose ranks on the Weird-O-Meter.

"Something to drink?" she asks, recovering nicely.

Half an hour later, having learned nothing from the experience, I'm at it again. A manicure this time. I use the fine flathead for a first pass under my nails and the leather bore to get to those hard-to-reach places. So far, so good. The large locking flathead is just the thing for an initial assault on the cuticles, followed by the scraping blade to clean up the rough parts left behind. This is actually going quite well. But we hit an air pocket or something just as I am applying pressure, and the scraping blade bites into my thumb. Like everything else on a multitool, it's sharper than it seems at first. I stick my thumb in my mouth to stop the bleeding, then figure that my rum and Coke is a better alternative. The alcohol will kill germs, and the ice will shrink the busted capillaries.

Anybody with an ounce of sense would have stopped there, but it was a long flight. Unfortunately, multitools have no specific implement for hangnails. So I choose to use the serrated portion of the knife blade at a 90-degree angle to the hangnails — for safety — and sort of abrade them off. This appears to work pretty well, and I'm on my third one when the guy playing Slave Zero next to me attempts a particularly fast evasive move and bumps my elbow. I now have wounds in nose, thumb, and ring finger.

At this point, some slight change in cabin pressure sets all three of my cuts bleeding. I go back to the bathroom and wrap my injured digits in toilet paper and pack my nostril with more toilet paper to stanch the flow. After the plane lands, I work my way down the aisle, multitool in its holster, me swathed in toilet tissue, looking like a mummy that's been in a fight. At the door is the attendant who was working the beverage cart.

"Bye-bye, now, sir," she says. Then she takes my arm and whispers, "The gate agent outside can direct you to the nearest medical station."

Don't Even Ask About My Turkey Season

This has not been my best spring gobbler season. With a week left, I have been out 11 times and fired my gun exactly not at all. In fact, the same three No. 4s have been in and out of my autoloader so often it looks like some demented midget has taken a ball-peen hammer to the brass. My six-pocket pants in this year's must-have camo, Realtree Hardwoods 20-200, have a newly installed rip next to the fly. I'm proud to say I can now work a friction call and pee at the same time. There are weepy poison-ivy blisters on both of my arms and the right rear quadrant of my head. Everywhere else is territory being fought over by DEET-resistant factions of the chigger and mosquito kingdoms.

It didn't start out this way, of course. I began the season comparing taxidermists' rates for a flying gobbler mount and wondering which corner of my office might afford the best light to show off its imposing length of beard and spur. Failure? Unthinkable. I had too much stuff to fail. There was the vest with padded back and more pockets than a pool table. There were the eight diaphragm calls that fit into nifty slanted boxes. Friction calls in slate, glass, and aluminum. Strikers of hickory, acrylic, and carbon. I had box calls, a gobbler tube, calls imitating the owl, hawk, woodpecker, and crow. I had two face masks and three sets of gobbler gloves. Jake and hen decoys that looked like brown Fruit Roll-ups when stowed. I had turkey socks. I even had one of those padded gun rests you buckle to your knee so that when you finally stand up to retrieve your bird you fall right down again and injure your hip. Failure? Not bloody likely.

Dawn on the season opener found me at the edge of a field, listening. At six o'clock, I raised the owl call to my lips and hooted. A gobbler answered up the ridge, sounding like some mad devil banging on a xylophone of human vertebrae. Heart pounding, I took off after him. At my first step, a stupendous gobbler flapped calmly out of the tree almost directly overhead and flew silently down the mountain. It was an omen I chose to ignore. But I never did hear or see the other bird again.

Seven more fruitless days afield passed. I did manage to call in a box turtle. I made him 20 feet out and watched him steadily close the distance to 16 over the course of an hour. He had little red eyes and seemed to be trying to tell me something, his jaw working soundlessly.

Throwing caution and wallet to the wind, I booked a three-day hunt at the Fort Lewis Lodge in the hills of southern Virginia with a different guide each day. My first was Frank, a certified mountain man, 6-foot-4 with flaming red hair and a beard you could have stashed a set of flatware in.

Frank is serious about turkeys. He not only hunts all 35 days of the season but also goes out 25 mornings straight before it opens to locate birds. Frank's a big believer in black cotton sewing thread to make his decoys bob up and down like they're feeding. "It's deadly," he promised. We got on a bird early and worked it for three hours, moving five times. On the bird's last gobble before shutting up for good, Frank said, "Ah think ah know that bird. That's one smart old gobbler. He's just jerkin' our chain."

My second guide — I'm not making this up — was an Amway salesman. No turkeys, but he did offer me some excellent cleaning products at competitive prices.

My scheduled guide for the last day had to cancel at the last minute, so I ended up hunting with the local preacher. "I've done 14 funerals so far this spring," he told me. "I *need* to go turkey hunting." About 11 o'clock, we were blind calling on top of a mountain when a gobbler answered. He pointed to a tree for me to set up by, then double-timed it 20 yards away to set up the decoys. Halfway back, the bird gobbled again, closer. I got my special knee pad buckled, my gun in position, and tried to stop shaking. Just as the preacher reached the tree and was sitting down, the bird made us, putted, and ran off. The preacher and I exchanged heartsick looks. "My fault," he said.

"I can't believe that bird came in so quick," he said. I managed a weak smile.

"Hey, that's turkey hunting," I tried to say cheerfully. I staggered to my feet and promptly fell down.

GPS:
GLOBAL
PERPLEXING SYSTEM

I have in my hand a small, gray electronic instrument that is revolutionizing the way sportsmen navigate the woods and waters, enabling us to get lost with greater precision than our forefathers ever dreamed possible. It's a GPS, which I purchased after a friend claimed that any idiot could learn to use it. I have since concluded that I'm not just any idiot and GPS stands for Global Perpetuation of Stupidity.

I was suspicious of the thing at first. For starters, it looks like an electric razor with an LCD display in its side and weighs in at a whopping 6 ounces. Nevertheless, this baby contains more stuff than I take on extended camping trips: a 12-channel, full-function electronic system that tracks 24 satellites orbiting Earth. (The satellites are reputed to be 11,000 nautical miles overhead, whizzing around the planet at 1.8 miles per second in six different paths.

When the unit locks on to three satellites, it can give your position to within 60 feet or so. With four satellites, it can tell your elevation. With five satellites, it advises you on lure selection, determines whether you have any outstanding parking tickets, and tells you if you are harboring the hanta virus.)

It has an antenna, electronic compass, and barometric altimeter, a computer that records 500 waypoints, an automatic track log that leaves electronic "bread crumbs," and a routing system that lets you navigate up to 50 waypoints in sequence. By my count, that much equipment ought to weigh about 6,000 pounds.

The GPS can tell you where you are, where you're headed, and where you've been. It can tell you how fast you're traveling (current, maximum, and average speeds), how far to your destination, how many feet you've climbed or descended, and when the sun will rise and set. The map scale is adjustable from 200 feet to 800 miles. The only thing the unit lacks is a meat thermometer.

For some outdoorsmen, this may give peace of mind. In my own case what the GPS provided — with the help of Evan, the 10-year-old down the street — was a large dose of confusion laced with humiliation.

Evan rapidly explained the satellite, map, pointer, elevation, and menu pages, each of which has an endless number of subpages within it containing options, settings, and cryptic phrases like *Timbalai 194* and *Afgooye.*

"Let's say you want to create a waypoint," Evan said, pushing buttons until a little electronic man on one knee appeared in the LCD. He was carrying a flag with the number 018 on it. Inside the flag was another little flag perched atop a tiny square. There was also a bubble over his head that said "OK?" I could not have been more intimidated by a pistol jabbed into my ear.

Evan dropped his voice as if speaking to a toddler: "We could just accept that and enter OK, but there are 28 other waypoint symbols we could choose to mark where we are." He hit another button and began scrolling through them: a car, house, tepee, fish, skull and crossbones, skull without crossbones, square, sinking ship, airplane, dollar sign, etc. He selected the house symbol and was about to proceed to confuse me even further when I snatched the unit from him and put a hand to my ear.

"I think I hear your momma calling you," I said. He looked puzzled. "I didn't hear anything," he said. I pretended to listen intently. "Ah. There she is again. You better get home. She sounds mad."

Seized by a mad desire to create an electronic bread-crumb trail, I fiddled with the thing and eventually got the compass to work, entered my house as a waypoint, and set off for a long walk around the block. When I got home, I discovered that I'd hardly moved at all, much less left bread crumbs. That's when I noticed the map scale was set to 800 miles. Some people say the day is coming when we'll all be using GPS whenever we venture into unknown territory. I say *Afgooye.*

Gear You Really, Really Need

Do you consider yourself a serious hunter? Take this pop quiz. Which of the following statements is a hunter *least likely* to utter on his deathbed?

(A) That monster buck I missed back in '71? He was really an inside-the-ears 6-pointer.

(B) I always secretly thought *The Bridges of Madison County* was Eastwood's best movie.

(C) I really wish I hadn't bought so much hunting gear.

If you guessed *C,* you win a pair of Mossy Oak Blaze Tree-Stand briefs. A real hunter may admit he stretched the truth, may harbor strange aesthetic opinions, but he knows that *too much gear* is an oxymoron, like saying a deer has *too big antlers*. My basement is so crammed with the stuff —

new, classic, useful, and ridiculous — that my wife, Jane, now requires an escort to take laundry down there. Below are a few items that you simply must have.

Adults-Only Deer Gear

The newest must-have whitetail accessory is — fasten your seat belts — buck semen! That's right! Not real buck semen, of course. That would be . . . unsemenly. Not to mention dangerous to collect. (What would you do? Dress up like a doe and take a test tube with you into the pen?) No, what we're talking about here is synthetic semen. We hunters will be buying railroad cars of the stuff this year.

According to the promotional literature of its distributors (the product is being offered by a number of companies), the "authentic odor and appearance of the product" will be obvious to "every male hunter." I may be a minority of one, but this male hunter has extremely limited experience with the sight or smell of buck semen. Frankly, I'd just as soon keep it that way. The manufacturers assure me, however, that synthetic buck semen works on two levels: (1) Its irresistible sexual appeal stimulates a mature buck's mating instinct; and (2) A little synthetic semen deposited in another buck's territory is "the ultimate insult." I would not recommend hunting on the ground with this stuff until more data is gathered on how angry bucks react to the ultimate insult at close range, but I think we can all agree that the chemists who formulated this stuff should be short-listed for next year's Nobel Prize.

I Need This Like I Need . . .
Eye protection is extremely important to hunters and fishermen, because if you lose your vision you've lost a very important part of your eyesight. Also, very few catalogs come in Braille. That's why Scott goggles with flexible thermofoam gaskets come not only in regular and over-the-glasses styles but also in clear and high-contrast sienna lenses. But the good people at Scott know that the discerning ATV rider or bass-boat jockey is always on the lookout for that "extra something." So, for just $49.95 ($16 more than the regular model), you can get its one-way Hologram Goggles, available in your choice of a single pattern: Bullet Holes.

That's right. You, the wearer, see normally when you've got these babies strapped to your head. To the world, however, you're sporting three really big bullet holes (caliber is not specified but looks to be about .30/

06) in your goggles. These quality optics virtually guarantee you the right-of-way in the marina or at crowded trailheads. The invisible-to-the-wearer feature means that you are likely to forget to take them off in public. This can result in priority seating at diners and restaurants and helps make that all-important first impression when requesting to hunt private property.

Ahem

I am of the firm belief that you can't have too much stuff slung around your neck in a deer stand. That's why — in addition to binocs, a grunt tube, laser rangefinder, and a lucky Mr. T medallion — I have added the Original Cough Muffler. This gem features washable, reusable filters, a non-glare matte finish, and its own lanyard. You just hack away into the mouthpiece whenever the urge hits, and it sucks up the sound. It's only $21.95, plus shipping and handling, from Ellington and Rush Hunting Products in Loganville, Georgia. The problem with this product is it sets you thinking: What about those coughs that come out from, you know, your other end? Aren't they far more likely to ruin your deer hunt? I think it's time somebody came up with a Below-the-Belt Cough Muffler — preferably one that wouldn't hurt to sit on.

Hey! My License Plate!
While we're on the subject, no hunting rig is complete without Uncle Booger's Bumper Dumper. (Actual motto: "When it comes to #2, we are #1.") Say good-bye to squatting behind a bush, in a flimsy Porta Potti, or in spider-infested outhouses with the Bumper Dumper (only $59.95). Just plug the sturdy frame and toilet seat into your trailer hitch, and you're good to go! The seat has been tested to an impressive 600 pounds, more than adequate for the average sportsman. You can use the Bumper Dumper with plastic sacks, most 5-gallon buckets, or a sealable bucket beneath the toilet seat.

Turn your vehicle into a rolling outhouse. Think of the pride you'll feel when visiting new friends for dinner, and they start to show you where the bathroom is. That's the moment you jerk a thumb toward your truck in the driveway and say, "Thanks anyway. Brought my own." Best results obtained with a stationary vehicle.

Fetch! Fetch! *Fetch!*
No hours are more precious than the ones you spend with your dog. This includes time spent throwing stuff to him in the water as

you prepare for another season freezing in the duck or goose blind. Sure, you can throw plastic dummies to your dog. But plastic dummies are cheap, and don't think your best friend doesn't know it. Closed-cell foam with a sewn-in polyrope for easier throwing is a step up. But nothing says "I wuff you" to your best friend like the time-tested Dokken's Dead Fowl Trainer. The soft, durable foam body simulates the look, feel, and weight of a dead bird. And the limp, totally free-swinging head discourages shaking. In fact, it practically shouts, *Take it easy, big fella! I'm dead already!* to your dog. The Canada goose is a mere $49.99, the mallard just $26.95.

As long as you've gone this far, you'll want to enhance the realism even more with the Dead Fowl Trainer Shark, an attachable wing that stands up vertically in the water and looks remarkably like a shark fin. It's just the ticket for building a young dog's confidence or working on multiple retrieves. Sadly, it may encourage your dog to attempt to retrieve actual sharks. Dokken's regrets that it cannot be liable for replacement dogs in such cases.

I know what you're thinking. *Hey, it gets tiring chucking fake dead birds out there!* It sure does. That's why you'll want to be able to launch them a cool 200 feet with the .22-caliber-blank-powered Retrieve-R-Trainer. The complete kit, manufactured by Specialty Products, includes the launcher, a two-piece shoulder stock, a foam dummy, a cleaning kit, and case for $129.99. Never mind that 200 feet is way beyond shotgun range. The real reason to buy this is to mess with your dog's head. About the time he's getting used to the idea that birds fall down (occasionally) when you shoot, show him you also have the power to raise the dead the same way. Your pup will look at you with new respect the very first time you use it. That's something you can't put a price tag on.

The Only Way to Hunt 'Em

Every year I vow to go bowhunting with less equipment. Every year I end up with more. And every year it helps me screw up in new and exciting ways.

I checked my cherished Mathews compound: newly installed Limb Savers, 7-inch Doinker stabilizer, and Meprolight tritium pins that glow in the dark. I set my rubber boots in a bag by the front door so I wouldn't forget them. Into my backpack went a rangefinder, binocs, tree belt with extra hooks, and an adjustable grunt tube that mimics everything from Barry White in heat to Minnie Mouse on helium. I stuffed in my hat, extra fleece vest, and peanut-butter sandwich (double bagged to prevent odor leakage). Then came a spray bottle of Scent Killer for on-stand touch-ups, folding saw, a small water bottle and big pee bottle (make sure not to mix these two up).

In the fanny pack I loaded a flashlight,

insect repellent, two Fletchunter releases (they're black, and I live in terror of dropping one and having to start a brush fire to find it), a bottle of wind indicator powder wrapped with 20 feet of orange tracking tape, knife, deer drag, rubber butchering gloves, disposable plastic scent-placing gloves, a bottle of Trail's End #307 along with six new scent wicks and reflective ties with which to hang them, arm guard, and license. There was probably some other essential stuff that I can't remember offhand, but that's most of it.

I went to bed that night at 10 and woke every half hour until my alarm finally went off at 4:30. There were a few cars already parked when I got to the woods, but nobody near my secret spot. I got upwind of the car and began to dress.

It was at this point I discovered I'd left my rubber boots standing at attention by the front door. I looked down at my shoes: 6-year-old orange leatherette bedroom slippers with vinyl soles that I can locate in the morning by smell alone.

There was only one thing to do. A $250 activated charcoal suit up top doesn't mean diddly when your feet smell like catfish bait. I got back in the car, sprayed down both slippers with half the bottle of Scent Killer, cranked the defroster on high, and crammed them in the vents. Ten minutes later, I began picking my way stealthily up the slope — falling on my face every 10 yards thanks to the vinyl soles and jamming the top of my tree stand into the back of my skull each time. I'd enhanced my camo with about 5 pounds of dirt by the time my flashlight beam found the single Bright Eye tack in my tree.

I was soon 20 feet up with an arrow nocked and the tattered remnants of hope fluttering in my heart. A groundhog waddled by at eight. At nine, a cardinal perched in a tree and looked at me funny. "Forgot my damn boots," I whispered. "Leave me alone."

At 9:30, a pair of small bucks appeared, a 4-pointer followed by a 6. They were working their way right into the wind and past my stand. I stood, legs shaking in my wet slippers, grunted once to stop them after they passed, and made an 18-yard quartering-away shot on the 6-pointer. He went down 70 yards away.

At the local processor's, I tried to keep the counter between the two of us as I asked for mostly steaks and burgers, with one ham to be made into jerky. I'd tucked the ticket in my wallet and was headed for the door when he caught me. "Hey, man," he called. "I see them shoes you got." I braced myself for the coming taunt. Instead, there was respect in his voice. "Still-hunter, right? You must know your onions to get one that way on opening day."

I turned and beamed at the guy. "Only way to hunt 'em," I said. Whereupon I swaggered out the door, hit a potato-chip wrapper in the parking lot, fell on my butt, and came up smiling. A very lucky season so far.

CONFESSIONS OF A BASS FISHERMAN

I've been peppering the bank methodically for a good half hour with a soft jerkbait when I catch something out of the corner of my eye. Thirty yards away, a single stalk in an isolated clump of reeds wags once in the breeze and comes back to attention. Only there is no breeze. And no stray puff of air would do a surgical strike on one reed. "Bass," I mutter, already stashing the rod noiselessly in the bottom of the canoe and lifting my window-sash anchor. Smooth as a shoplifter, I take up the paddle. Three quiet J-strokes put me in casting position.

The rest unfolds like the money shot in a *Monster Hawgs of Transylvania* video. I throw 10 feet past the target and tease the plastic back like the day's blue-plate special. The reed bends again. A sudden hole opens in the water. The lure falls down it. And then I'm into him, a bass like I've never fought before: too big to jump, too mad to think, too wild to care.

The first surge nearly pulls the rod from my hand. Then he's dragging the boat up into a cove, the reel is choking each time he bucks, and I'm shaking and reeling frantically in between surges to try and keep up with him. Now his dorsal fin breaks the water, like the conning tower of a submarine surfacing. He looks like a very large fish — only bigger. If I can just hang on I'll have the bass of my life. He dives, and I'm trying everything I can think of to turn his head when my wife's face suddenly appears suspended in the air next to the canoe. She doesn't look happy to see me.

"Stop punching me in the back!" she snaps. "What the hell's wrong with you?"

I wake to find I'm in my own bed, arms pinned in a backlash of nightgown and bedsheets. I have been chasing dream bass again.

Bass fishermen aren't the craziest people in the world. We do not claim to be the pope, nor that the CIA has implanted tiny receivers in our teeth, nor that we know for a fact that Steven Seagal is a German dressmaker hiding out from his creditors as an action hero in Hollywood. On the other hand, you do not want to get between us and our vehicles when we are sneaking out of work to go fishing. It's just not a safe place to stand.

Some behaviorists say fishing is a form of obsessive-compulsive disorder. Cast, reel, repeat. Continue until your arm falls off. This is, of course, total nonsense. We will fish only until our arms are so sore we can no longer lift them. This is a big distinction.

Bass anglers will fish at any time, in any kind of weather, on any kind of water. One of my better fish last year came in deepest, darkest Washington, D.C., 20 yards from where half a dozen police cars, blue lights turning the night into a weird kind of funhouse, were haphazardly parked during a major drug bust at Hain's Point. I'd nailed a 4-pounder along a hydrilla bed on a Tiny Torpedo. One of the beefier cops squinted into the night as he herded men into a paddy wagon, saw my boat, and waddled over to the rail along the river. "Doing any good?" he asked. "I always wondered 'bout fishing here."

There's a reason for our devotion. It is this: Once you've had a day where it all comes together — when your casts could land on a marshmallow at 25 yards and you sense the fish sucking your lure in right before it happens and they're hungry for exactly what you're throwing — you suddenly feel like you're in exactly the spot you were meant to be, snugly in God's pocket. It doesn't happen very often, but when it does it's magic. The absolute chaos of your life suddenly makes sense, and you know firsthand that at least one path to grace can be navigated with a paddle, oars, or trolling motor.

And we will lie, if we must, to get to the water. Back before I realized I'd never make employee of the month and quit a regular job to take up the twin vows of outdoor writing and poverty, I spent as much time scheming to get out of work as I did actually working. Chronic ailments were my stock-in-trade. From May to October, I was beset by periodontal disease and sinus infections, sleep apnea and a back that required regular chiropractic adjustment. These conditions were aggravated by incoming low-pressure systems and the tidal variations of the river I fished.

My boss knew. Heck, the whole office knew. But knowing and proving are two different things. Walking to my car in the lot, I'd be so full of fishing anticipation that I'd have to force myself not to run. It was a heady feeling, to still be on the clock while surfing the crest of the first wave of rush-hour traffic, headed for a place called the

Stick-Ups and an afternoon chasing bass. Now that I'm my own boss and can go fishing whenever my wife says it's okay, I almost miss it. Almost.

Bass fishermen are not, as so often portrayed, equipment junkies. You give me a truck, boat, trailer, depthfinder, trolling motor, lights, GPS, radio, aerator, four tackle boxes, 100 lures, eight rods, and a pair of polarized glasses, and I'm one happy camper. A measly 70 grand would just about do it. Heck, I bet Ray Scott spent that much each year on those fringed cowboy jackets he used to wear at the Classic weigh-in before they gave him the boot. And despite our affection/affliction for gear, we also love knowing that the bass couldn't care less.

We know what George Washington Perry, the farm boy from Rentz, Georgia, was outfitted with when he caught The Fish, the 22-pound 4-ounce monster he dredged up from Lake Montgomery pond back in 1932. He was using a $1.33 baitcasting outfit and a Creek Chub Wiggle Fish, a wooden lure with glass eyes. He was fishing from a skiff he made himself from 75 cents worth of scrap lumber. That fish was very nearly spherical, 32 inches long and 28 inches in girth, only a little smaller than the bass in my dreams.

The new world-record largemouth is more than likely finning its way around someplace right now, scaring the bejesus out of any little 12-pounder that makes the mistake of settling into its hole. I want to be the one to catch it, of course. I want the million bucks in endorsements and the everlasting fame, and I want the world to be mesmerized by how humble I am afterward, thanking Jesus and Momma and my corporate sponsors.

But if I can't be the one, I hope it's some boy sitting on a bucket with a bobber and a worm, some kid who had to stay behind because there wasn't enough room for him in the boat. That might be the best thing to ever happen to modern bass fishing.

THE MIDDLE GROUND

In a country where fishing, like Mideast politics or women's fashion, has been taken over by the extremists, guys who take the middle path — the way of discount tackle shops, wet tennis shoes, poison ivy, and spinning gear — are accorded all the respect of carp chum.

Every so often, I venture out to see what the modern American bass and trout boys are up to. It nearly always confirms my opinion that if Missing the Point were a criminal offense, most of these guys would be making license plates.

My last excursion with a local bass fisherman illustrated this perfectly. I sank into the upholstery of his $22,000 raspberry flake rocket sled, outfitted with a trolling motor the size of my car's engine and 3D forward-looking sonar so sophisticated you can't sell one to anybody from Libya or France. My host wedged me in tight, looked over at me like you would at a baby in a car seat, and hit the throttle. The big outboard exploded like hell had opened a drive-thru window just behind us, the G-forces flattening out my cheeks. I realized we weren't on the water so much as above it, descending occasionally to punish it for getting in our way.

My host carried his own personal thicket of bait-casters, graphite broomsticks spooled with 20-pound-test so he could yank 3-pound bass out of the river's dense hydrilla. Once he hooked one, he brought it in so fast it looked like the fish was water-skiing headfirst toward the boat. He stopped casting only once in 9 hours, to wolf down a pack of peanut-butter crackers. I was surprised he took the time to unwrap them.

Then I made the mistake of asking if he ever used spinning rods. "Hell, no," he growled. "I call those fairy wands."

Now call it dumb luck or call it fate, but on that particular day the biggest bass, a 4-1/2-pounder, fell to a pumpkin tube on a 1/8-ounce slip sinker cast by yours truly, Tinkerbell. With his fairy wand.

At the other end of the scale are my yuppie friends who have taken up fly fishing with all the gaiety of Jehovah's Witnesses. Where did these people come from? I think what happens is this: If you make over

$80,000 a year and drive a Saab, somebody from the Fly Fishing Bureau of Indoctrination shows up at your house and teaches you to false cast in your living room. If you also wear steel-rimmed glasses and have an untrained golden retriever with a red bandana tied around its neck, they immediately present you with a Tonkin bamboo rod (two tips), a brain surgeon's headlamp, and a leather leader wallet embossed with Izaak Walton's profile.

At a party, one of these instant experts actually sniffed, "Of course you can catch more fish on a spinning rod . . ." leaving the sentence unfinished, which is a clever way of saying, ". . . unless you are a total moron" without moving your lips. I just nodded my head as if he had a good point and stuck my fist in the yogurt dip.

Then I got a little testy. "Wait a minute," I said as evenly as I could. "Did I miss something while I was in the bathroom? Was there a moment when catching less fish became more fun? I love catching more fish! Some of my best times fishing have actually occurred when I caught a lot of fish! What happens when you catch a lot of fish? DOES IT MAKE YOU SAD?" By now he was backing up as if he'd hooked a big gar in a small pool, and my girlfriend was rattling the car keys.

I most often see these guys heading up tiny creeks, muttering their catechism, "egg, larva, pupa, adult," while I'm walking down to bigger water. They end up on their hands and knees casting size 20 Pale Morning Duns to fish that began life in concrete pools, max out at 8 inches, and don't live through the summer. In a way, I admire these guys. What they do takes a lot of skill. On the other hand, so does knitting a hammock for a guinea pig out of dental floss. Doesn't mean I'm going to spend my weekend doing it.

I'll take the middle ground, thank you, and I won't apologize. The smallmouth is a 20-million-year-old wild American fish that first appeared in the Great Lakes. Around my part of the country, smallmouths live in the faster-moving sections of big rivers and fight like crazed bronze missiles. They've got more heart than largemouth bass and more power than brown trout. For all that, they're a democratic fish: cooperative enough that a young boy or girl with their first spin-cast rig can have fun, but challenging enough that even the best angler (spin or fly) can spend a lifetime hunting that thirteen-year-old 5-pounder. They do not get that old by being dumb and they do not go gentle.

Best of all, they have the sense to live where a fish should. If water could talk, and you took any sip of sleepy bass water or a drop of a hyper little trout stream (the kind that usually looks like it could be turned off if someone accidentally put a kink in the hose), then asked what it would like to be, the answer would be the same: a river. The remarkable thing is that rivers do talk: they murmur, gurgle, suck, and roar. Rivers are water at its prime, filled with purpose and urgency as they say their good-byes. I like their restlessness. I find it energizing.

I'm standing waist-deep in a Potomac River rock garden 23 miles from where the president ties up traffic for 15 minutes whenever he goes to the McDonald's on 17th Street. The star grass is tugging at my legs in the current as I cast to ancient ambush stations behind boulders, the ledges I know from years of donating lures there, the seams where dead water meets quick. I am the only person out here, and behind me a blood-red sunset is pulling mares' tails west over the roof of the world, and the swallows have come to wheel and sip bugs from the air.

I cast a silver Rapala — no satellite uplink, no quadrasonic propeller, no phosphorescent Hawg Scent — into an eddy, where it spins all woozy in the foam. I twitch it once, wait, then make it wobble like a drunk performing for the police.

You know the rest. There comes the dark shape rising, a concussion, the electricity in the rod that says, *I think somebody's home.*

He leaps twice, all shivering gills and anger, pulls line, and surges toward an undercut. I turn him and he heads right at me, thinks better of it, and makes a last run downstream for heavy water, where I turn him again. What finally comes into my hand is 14 inches, maybe a pound, nothing to brag about. But this is not about bragging. This is about something else entirely. I heft him for a better look: his wild eye, the mottled olive-and-bronze camo not yet available in stores, the body honed by a life in quick water. It has been too long since I've been out here. I've forgotten how vivid and undeniable these fish are, how no one has told them they're not fashionable this year. "*Achigan,*" I say, repeating the name Algonquin Indians had for him: *ferocious.*

I lower him back. He snaps from my hands and is gone. The river shoulders past, a busy man with other things on his mind. I fish on, catching several more. I don't even remember to keep count. Suddenly it's dark and I realize that for over an hour I've not thought once about my car's transmission, or that my boss came into my office this morning to brag about his son's putting an entire pizza in his mouth, or that the woman I'm seeing sometimes says she feels alone when she's with me. Guys need this. It's sort of what we have instead of a book club. I suddenly have the momentary and surprising feeling that at this moment I'm exactly where I'm supposed to be. I'm calm. I'm happy. I'm happier here than any place I can think of.

LILYFISH

After the world takes an eggbeater to your soul, you never know what's going to get you up and back among the living. In my case, it was the ham. It was 3:30 on a sweltering July afternoon, three weeks to the hour since my new baby daughter lay down for a nap and woke up on the other side of this life.

I decided it was time to go fishing. There were any number of good reasons. For one, I could still smell Lily's baby sweetness in the corners of the house, still feel her small heft in the hollow of my shoulder. For another, I'd hardly left the house since she died and had taken to working my way through an alarming amount of dark rum and tonic each night, not a sustainable grief management technique over the long haul. Jane and I had planted the memorial pink crepe myrtle and the yellow lilies, chosen for having the audacity to bloom in the heat of the summer, the very time Lily died.

But it was the ham that got me off the dime. After the funeral, the neighbors had started bringing over hogs' hind legs as if the baby might rise from the dead and stop by for a sandwich if they could just get enough cured pork in the refrigerator. I knew my mind wasn't quite right, knew I still hadn't even accepted her death. But it seemed like I'd lose it unless I put some distance between me and the ham.

I shoved a small box of lures in a fanny pack, spooled up a spinning rod with 6-pound mono line, and filled a quart bottle with tap water. On my way out the door, I stopped, as I have taken to doing since her death, to touch the tiny blue urn on the mantel. "Baby girl," I said. I stood there for several minutes, feeling the coolness of fired clay and waiting for my eyes to clear again. Then I got in the car and drove 20 miles north of D.C. to the Seneca Breaks on the upper Potomac River.

I didn't particularly care that it was 102 degrees outside. I didn't particularly care that any smallmouth bass not yet parboiled by the worst heat wave in memory would scarcely be biting. I was furious at the world and everything still living in it now that my daughter wasn't. As I drove, the radio reported severe thunderstorms to the west and said they might be moving our way. Fine by me. If someone up there wanted to send a little electroshock therapy my way, I'd be easy to find.

Even at five o'clock the sun still had its noon fury. The heat had emptied the normally crowded parking lot at the river's edge. I stepped out of the air-conditioned car into the afternoon's slow oven. I slugged down some water, put my long-billed cap on, found a wading stick in the underbrush, and walked into the river. The water was bathtub warm and 2 feet below normal. Seneca Breaks, normally a mile-long series of fishy-looking riffles and rock gardens, was, like the only angler fool enough to be out there, a ghost of its former self. At least it didn't smell like ham. But the fish weren't here, and I realized I shouldn't be either. It dawned on me that I'd better get in water that went over my waist or risk heatstroke.

Just upstream from the breaks, the river is called Seneca Lake, 3 miles of deep flats covered with mats of floating grass. I worked my way to the head of the breaks and slipped into this deeper water, casting a 4-inch plastic worm on a light sinker. Soon I'd waded out chin-deep into the lake, holding my rod arm just high enough to keep

the reel out of the water. There were bait-
fish dimpling the surface every so often and
dragonflies landing on my wrist, and once a
small brown water snake wriggled by so
close I could have touched him.

Nothing was hitting my worm, but that
was to be expected. My arms seemed to be
working the rod on their own, and I was
content to let them. I stood heron-still and
felt the slow current brush grass against my
legs. Every so often, a minnow would
pucker up and take a little nip at my exposed
leg. It tickled. Baby fish. I remembered how
I'd call her Lilyfish sometimes when changing her diaper, remembered how she had
loved to be naked and squiggling on the
changing table, gazing up at me and gurgling with something approaching rapture
as I pulled at her arms and legs to stretch
them.

The tears welled up again. I found the
melody to an old Pete Townshend song running circles through my head and finally
latched on to the chorus:

After the fire, the fire still burns,
The heart grows older but never ever learns.

That's how it was, all right. The fire was
gone, but it still burned. It would always
burn. The memories — her smell, her smile,
the weight of her in my arms — would

always smolder. And I'd always yearn for the one thing I'd never have.

And what struck me as I stood alone in the middle of the river was that while my world had been changed forever, the world itself had not changed a whit. The river simply went about its business. A dead catfish, bloated and colorless, washed serenely past, on its way back down the food chain. The sun hammered down and a hot wind wandered the water.

I caught a bluegill, then two little smallmouths, within 10 minutes of each other. As I brought the fish to the surface, I had the sensation of bringing creatures from a parallel universe into my own for a minute before sending them darting back home. I wondered if death might be like this, traveling to a place where you didn't think it was possible to breathe, only to arrive discovering that you could. I hoped it was. The older I get, the more I believe that there is such a thing as the soul, that energy changes form but still retains something it never loses. I hoped that Lily's soul was safe. That she knew how much she was still loved.

I don't know how long I stayed there or even if I kept fishing. I remember looking up at some point and noticing that the light had softened. It was after eight and the sun was finally headed into the trees. And now, just like every summer night for aeons, the birds came out: an osprey flying recon over the shallows 50 feet up; a great blue heron flapping deep and slow, straight toward me out of the fireball, settling atop a rock and locking into hunting stance. And everywhere swallows coming out like twinkling spirits to test who could trace the most intricate patterns in the air, trailing their liquid songs behind them.

Suddenly I wasn't angry anymore. This is the world, I realized for the millionth time, and its unfathomable mystery: always and never the same, composed in roughly equal parts of suffering and wonder, unmoved by either, endlessly rolling away. It was getting dark now, hard to see the stones beneath the water. I waded carefully back to my car, rested the stick by a post for another fisher-man to use, changed into dry clothes, and drove home.

Take your grief one day at a time, someone had told me. I hadn't known what he meant at the time, but I did now. This had been a good day. Lily, you are always in my heart.

THE BASS BOAT
BLUES

In late summer, when the sun turns the water into a sheet of hammered copper and I have calluses on each shoulder from humping my canoe from roof rack to river and back, the brochures begin to hatch. Slick as wet bonefish, they slide magically under the front door and flop open right to the centerfold: a soft-focus image of a naked 20-foot bass boat. She's a beauty all right, with a hull like Jennifer Lopez sporting twin 18-gallon antislosh live wells (the boat, I mean). There's a guy at the wheel, skimming across a mirror-smooth sundown lake at tremendous speed. His tanned face is mostly hidden behind the tinted cockpit windscreen and a fresh logo cap snugged down low. But you can see his mouth. And he's smiling a smile that says everything you need to know. *Hey, buddy, got me a real nice little rig here.*

And you don't.

77

Now I learned all about the heartbreak of pursuing girls you couldn't have way back in the sixth grade courtesy of Helen Carlsen, so I usually take the sensible route and transfer the catalogs immediately to the circular file. But the other night, one slipped into a pile of bills and followed me downstairs into the basement. The American basement — land of spiderwebs and old reel parts, furnace filters and mildewed sleeping bags — was once a safe haven for a man having a minor midlife crisis.

Within five minutes I had surfed onto the Web site in the ad and was halfway through the "Build This Boat" feature on a $30,500 bass boat (rigging and freight not included).

I couldn't help it. I've spent most of my adult fishing life with my butt planted on a cane seat in a boat that nearly capsizes every time a good-size duck paddles by. I was defenseless against the song of words like "three-across seating," "radar speed 64–68 miles per hour," and "trolling motor management panel enclosed in rear with 50-amp circuit breakers."

Suddenly, I was 12 years old and back on the playground being mesmerized by Helen Carlsen's impossibly blond hair and that sprinkling of freckles across the top of her nose. In short, I snapped.

For the most part, I plugged in the standard features: a 225-horse EFI engine with stainless prop, triple aerator-fill pumps with timers, front bike seat with power pedestal, and pilot and partner cup holders. Nothing fancy. And since I wanted my wife to enjoy the boat, too, I picked out the most Martha Stewart-like colors: Mica Mist for the carpet, Mocha Frost aft deck accents, Moondust vinyl seats. Fifty-eight gallons of gas seemed sufficient, as did a maximum capacity of four people.

But then I clicked on over to the options page. A spare tire, galvanizing job on the trailer, and surge brakes on the second axle added $925. A tournament-level depth-finder was another grand. But I swear I don't know how the carpet embroidery ($215), Hot Foot throttle control ($100), or keel protectors ($300) got on there.

By the time I got the boat loaded and headed to check-out, I was looking at $33,916. Assuming I could scrape together $1,000 for a down payment and hold out for $500 in trade for my canoe (it's still in really good shape after nine years), I was looking at 36 easy payments of, well, let's just forget about the whole damn thing.

Instead, I swept out the workroom. I oiled all my reels, reorganized my tackle boxes, even got down on my knees with a bent coat hanger and fished out the stray socks underneath the dryer. About the time I'd worked up a good sweat and figured the worst was over, the phone rang. It was Jim, wanting to go fishing Saturday.

"What time Saturday?" I asked.

"Hey, man, whatever time you want. You the one with the canoe."

Suddenly, I felt a whole lot better.

THE LATE,
LATE SHOW

Late January, 12 degrees and falling, the northwest wind hurrying a red sun toward its slot in the horizon. Seated in a gently rocking tree stand 70 yards back from a field of winter wheat, I am exploring that fine line between hunting really hard and suicide by hypothermia. A hunter may take either a buck or doe during the late bow season in my state, and any guy with half a brain should be happy with either by this point in the game. Me, I'm holding out for a buck, a good one. Might as well go down swinging.

In a feeble attempt to stave off the cold, I've shoved hand warmers inside my gloves and toe warmers into my boots. I've been trying to ignore the shivers by reading the plastic wrappers they come in. These marvels of modern technology consist of stuff that has been around since the wheel: iron, water, activated carbon, and salt. In French, the other language on the wrapper, this is

81

translated as *fer, eau, carbone active, et sel.*

Nevertheless, the package contains more warnings than a new chain saw. The warmers are not to be applied directly to bare skin, desensitized skin, on the instep (*cou-de-pied*), ankle (*la cheville*), or arch (*l'arche du pied*). Do not use them when sleeping. Children, the elderly, and some disabled people should be supervised when using the product. Don't put them on frostbite. Don't puncture them. If you do, resist the temptation to place the contents in your eyes or mouth. Don't swallow them. If you do, consult a physician. Fast.

In direct violation of the safety instructions I have duct-taped a fifth and larger warmer directly against my skull beneath two hats. I have been doing this for years, no doubt slowly cooking my brain. This explains why I'm (a) bow-hunting in late January and (b) holding out for a decent buck.

The strange fact is that I like the late season, cold and all. I like it because the smart hunters — those smug guys diligent enough to scout the preseason and disciplined enough to avoid overhunting prime stands — have tagged out. That leaves the woods to guys like me: the obsessed, the unhinged, the ones who don't know when to quit. There is a strange satisfaction in this kind of hunting. If you get a deer, the victory is that much sweeter. If not, it damn sure wasn't for lack of trying.

At 5:22, I spot a doe 100 yards out as she picks her way toward the field. As long as she's moving, I can see her. The moment she stops, she disappears into the landscape. Despite years of seeing it, the trick still fascinates. At 5:34, I register a little 4-pointer in the distance. His unusually white antlers almost glow in the fading light. I don't want to shoot him; I want to warn him. I want to tell him to muddy those stickers up if he hopes to make it through another year.

At 5:52, legal light ends, but something keeps me on stand, watching. Then he comes, the big shape ghosting in from upwind. It's too dark to read my watch, let alone count tines, but I know this is the one, know it as surely as if I were seeing him under a spotlight on an empty stage. I know it because my heart is booming and the heart does not lie on late January afternoons when it's 12 degrees out. The world stops as he passes soundlessly beneath my stand, as he enters the dark field to feed. Suddenly, for the first time all day, I notice that I'm warm all over. And a strange rapture courses through me, every molecule in my hunter's blood suddenly alive and singing.

■ ■ ■ ■

II
LYING,
HALLUCINATING, AND
COVETING GEAR YOU
DON'T NEED:
BECOMING A REAL
OUTDOORSMAN

■ ■ ■ ■

Too Long at the Funhouse

Beware the corn dog. It is a fickle friend, one that can turn on you without warning. The first one at the sportsman's expo had gone down so well that I opted for a second. An hour later, watching from the bleachers as a bass pro flipped a jig to a dozen bored-looking largemouths in a tank the size of a tractor trailer, that second dog turned around and bit me. My brow was damp, despite a room temperature of 55 degrees, which is about as warm as it gets on a February day inside a ramshackle brick cow palace dating from the early 1900s. And the hall seemed to be tilting a little to one side. I knew the signs: I'd stayed too long at the funhouse.

Realizing that the hall's only men's room was probably a quarter mile away and hidden behind one of the exhibits for the raffle items I hadn't won — the Hummer with the zebra-stripe paint job or the shotgun worth two years of college tuition — I decided to sit tight and see which stopped moving first, the room or my stomach.

The bass angler sat 12 feet up in a folding chair at one end of the narrow tank. It may well have been an informative talk. Between the acoustics of the place and a guy working the sound board who looked like one of Black Sabbath's original roadies, what I understood was the following: "Ahm gahm zep issa hegol bass wiffem no belay rat cheer inna ma blibe well. Heh heh heh."

I sat there until the seminar was over and everyone else had drifted away. I watched the bass suspended in the tank until I realized we were operating at about the same level of consciousness. Then I climbed down from the bleachers with the caution usually reserved for tree-stand descents in the dark and began the long walk out. I passed the fly-fishing expert dropping a Yellow Humpy into a Dixie cup 75 feet away. A mannequin in a Rancho Safari gillie suit suddenly came to life as I walked by, grabbing me in a bear hug and nearly scaring me out of my shoes. Progress through the crowd halted near the platform where the Lumberjills, an all-female logging group, were performing. I never saw the ladies, but I heard chain saws bellowing like dueling Harleys, smelled the freshly cut wood, and saw, every so often, a 3-pound double-bit axe go spinning above the crowd and land with a solid *whunk* in a target 20 feet away. A burly guy with forearms like hams and a pencil stuck up under his cap rubbed his chin in a worried manner. "Helluva show," he said to his buddy. "But I ain't 100 percent sure I'd want my wife to be that handy with an axe, 'specially during the season."

Outside, the winter sun had left orange and purple skid marks in the sky. Above them dark mare's tails danced slowly, caught the last light, and lit up briefly.

My car was parked by a little strip of scrub woods. As I was unlocking it, I noticed an opening a few feet away. The tracks in the black mud were fresh. I hunched down and entered the woods, the faintest breeze in my face. Ten minutes and 20 yards later, I saw them. A doe and her two offspring ghosted across another trail not 30 yards ahead of me. I held my breath and watched their shapes filter through the near-darkness, members of an ancient race who knew nothing of sportsman's shows and everything about the earth's secrets.

Back at the car, I breathed in some more of the cold winter air. My head was clear.

My heart had begun to beat normally again. Two hours later I pulled into the driveway. "How was the show?" my wife asked. "Oh, you know, awful," I said. "But the parking lot was great." She didn't respond at first. But a few minutes later, she said, "You look tired. You oughta go to bed." I did and was asleep in moments, following as deer moved through woods in the darkness.

Rut Strategies
for the
Married Hunter

I think I have finally isolated the most important difference between whitetail bucks and the guys who hunt them. According to deer biologists, the mature whitetail is an essentially social animal (it communicates with other deer year-round by leaving scent) that prefers to spend the great majority of its time alone. The mature whitetail hunter, on the other hand, is most comfortable alone in the deer woods, but is compelled to spend most of his time in society.

If you think about it, we and the deer are really sort of mirror images of each other, and this phenomenon extends to the rut. In the whitetail's world, it is the female who dictates when the rut starts. In the domain of the deer hunter, on the other hand, the female is often the one to decide when the rut hunt ends. This year, for example, my hunting ended on November 14 at 11:32

a.m. when my wife — in a nonverbal but unmistakable manner — declared it over.

Don't get me wrong. I wouldn't go back to being single on a bet. The benefits to the human male of marriage are well known. If forced to choose between my marriage and deer hunting, I would pause only long enough to gnash my teeth, wipe the tears from my eyes, and give fond good-bye pats to a Winchester .270, a Knight .50 muzzle-loader, and a Mathews compound bow. Thing is, I don't want to have to choose. I would be very happy with both.

But the married deer hunter must adapt, adjust, and improvise to hunt the rut effectively. Farewell, endless summer evenings glassing likely areas to see if there are any good bucks there. Adieu, early-fall days afield pinpointing food sources, doe bedding areas, and the funnels that connect them. And remember when you could hang 11 stands to account for differing wind directions? Those days have gone bye-bye.

Why? Because the most important element of rut-hunting preparation for the married hunter is building up a reservoir of goodwill against the toll of the coming season. October finds this woodsman taking his spouse out to dinner more often than he can afford, volunteering for double baby duty on weekends, and even attempting to cook dinner.

In recent years, I have made the ultimate sacrifice to fill the reservoir: forgoing *Monday Night Football* so that Jane and I can watch another riveting episode of *Ally McBeal* together. (Unfortunately, three of my single hunting buddies have found this out and now take particular delight in placing a conference call to me on Tuesday morning. "Man, Raiders killed the Broncos last night, 38–28," they'll say. "Great game. But, listen, the real reason we called is to ask if you think Ally and that cute guy in accounting are gonna get something going or what?" Then they all laugh so hard they start to weep.)

Jane does not pretend to understand why I have to be in the woods in November, but she tries to be patient. Even her patience has an end, however, and this year the end came on November 14. That morning I had glassed a wide 8-pointer chasing a doe into a thicket and had come home just long enough to shower and put on fresh camo before returning to the woods.

In retrospect, it occurs to me that I may not have actually spoken to my wife for four days, which could have been the precipitating factor. While I was lathering up with scent-killing soap, a familiar woman's hand appeared wordlessly inside the shower curtain. In the palm of that hand sat a baby, who was grinning up at me as water darkened her pink terry-cloth onesie. I took my daughter, whose diaper was heavy and odorous. I heard the door to the bathroom click shut. I looked at my watch. It said 11:32. At that moment, the rut had just ended.

There's always next year.

DEATH (NEARLY) BY BASS FISHING

In a moment of acute midlife irresponsibility a few months back, I decided to roll the dice, plunking down four grand I didn't actually have to chase giant peacock bass in Brazil. Peacocks, native to the Amazon Basin, have a lifelong case of road rage and gleefully destroy anything that gets in their way, big topwater lures included. They are bass in the same way that Komodo dragons are lizards. More than one Yankee angler has gone home minus a thumb after trying to lip a fish with razors in its mouth.

My plan was to go to a fishing camp on the Rio Negro, about 1,000 miles upstream of Belém, at the mouth of the Amazon. This is where the current world-record speckled peacock (largest of the nine known species), a 27-pounder, came from.

All was going well until just before my last connection, when I was poleaxed by a combination of nausea, dizziness, diarrhea, fever, chills, and vomiting. Also, I didn't feel very well. I must have hailed a taxi before passing out, because I woke sweaty and feverish in a bed at the Hilton in Belém.

Flexibility is the key to successful foreign travel. I immediately decided against fishing in favor of a more important mission: attaining the minibar at the foot of the bed before I died. Everything that was crucial to my survival was inside that magic box, including potable water to combat the dehydration that had made me delirious and transformed my tongue into a twice-baked potato; little boxes of fruit juice to replace the calories that had been rocketing out of my body; and Chivas Regal miniatures to muffle the auto-body shop that had taken up residence behind my forehead.

In a single, athletic move, I lurched forward and fell face first into the shag carpet at the foot of the bed. It was soft and, I assume, synthetic, since it seemed to wick the sweat away from my skin. At eye level, the tangled fibers turned into an aerial view of the rain forest. In the ensuing fever dream, I found myself floating, looking down into dense jungles that had never seen an axe. Green and yellow birds did a stately, hopping dance by bright rivers. Monkeys solemnly inspected fruit in the tops of trees.

Jaguars traced ancient paths known only to their race. Somewhere in the wispy clouds, Sting was plucking a guitar and singing sorrowfully in Portuguese. It was then that I understood that the rain forest was truly the lungs of the world. Or at least of this particular shag carpet.

The hotel doctor who saw me was a very wise man with a long face. He listened to my chest, told me I was indeed sick, and left a $100 charge on my room bill. Two days later, recovered enough to fly home, I sat for an hour in the stifling heat of Belém by the docks of the river, watching three little boys fishing in the muddy water. Their technique was to cram a crust of bread into a wine bottle, tie it to some heavy mono, and cast out. Five minutes later, they would dive into the river and follow the lines down to their bottles, trapping the minnows inside with the palm of a hand. They pantomimed to me that they would eat the fish, bones and all, in soups their mothers would make that evening.

So that was my South American adventure: four grand and 6,000 miles to sit on a bench and watch kids catch minnows. On the other hand, I'd cheated death, reached the minibar under extreme conditions, and learned a new way to fish. And I'd been reminded of a lesson I seem destined to relearn every few years: When you roll the dice on a dream trip, make sure you've got a bottle of Kaopectate within easy reach.

STIR CRAZY

The instant the babysitter shows up, all you're going to see of me is taillights. I've got an accomplice, Jim, idling at the nearest ramp in a bass boat with a new sonar unit. I've got six rods ready and stashed in my car, along with some heavy bass ordnance from the new Cabela's catalog: Recoil Grubs made of a miracle plastic that stretches to 15 times its original size so that a 4-inch bait doubles as a cargo tie-down in emergencies. Yamamoto Senkos, those pricey little jerkbaits packed with so much salt that you're tempted to snack on them yourself when the fishing's slow. The Yo-Zuri Hardcore Shad with the tungsten weight that slides to the tail of the lure for long casts and then falls into the belly, where it is secured by a tiny trapdoor during the retrieve.

This stuff is burning a hole in my tackle bag. I have not been fishing for an entire week, ever since my wife went to Chicago on a business trip. But today the dry spell ends. Faith, the high school girl up the street, has agreed to babysit. Sensing my desperation, she has also jacked her rate up to six bucks an hour. Fine. If I ignore the speed limit, I can be waterborne in 16 minutes. But the green flag doesn't drop until Faith shows.

Meanwhile, Emma and I are watching *The Lion King* on video for the 6,000th time. At 3, Emma lives in a blissfully simple world. The first thing she wants upon waking is a bottle of milk. The second is *The Lion King.* Right now, we're at Emma's absolute favorite part. Timon, the fast-talking meerkat, and Pumbaa, his dim-witted but lovable sidekick (a warthog with a flatulence problem), have just encountered Simba, the runaway lion cub who wrongly believes he is responsible for his father's death. Meerkat and warthog welcome lion into their carefree outcast existence with the insanely catchy song that (after much repetition) winds up:

It's our problem-free phi-los-o-phy.
Hakuna Matata!

Emma squeals, "Kuna Tata!" and I check my watch. Faith is now 11 minutes overdue. I look around the room for something to

100

place between my jaws in case I start to scream involuntarily.

Things were not always thus. There was a time just a few years ago when I fished whenever I wanted. I generally chose those times by the positions of the moon and sun, and by relative barometric pressure. I liked dawn or dusk, a low (or at least falling) barometer, and the moon either directly underfoot or overhead. As much as possible, I avoided weekends, which is when people who work for a living fish. I was, to put it bluntly, an unbearably smug bass fisherman. Fatherhood has taken me down a few pegs. These days, I take my fishing whenever I can get it, and I take it humbly.

The phone rings. It's Faith. She says she has a sore throat and can't make it. End of story. I call Jim on his cell.

"I got nuked," I tell him. "Babysitter's sick."

In the background I hear the sounds of truck doors slamming, the eager voices of anglers loading up their gear, the bittersweet Doppler whine of a boat engine as it heads off into the distance toward fish. Meanwhile, Emma is rewinding the tape so she can watch her favorite scene again.

"I feel your pain, bud," Jim says, and I know it's not just a Bill Clinton imitation.

He's a father, too. His daughter is now 16. He once again fishes at will.

"Next time," he tells me.

"Yeah," I say. "Hakuna Matata."

He laughs. "Oh, man. *The Lion King.* That sure takes me back. You know what? I actually got to where I liked that movie."

I quietly hang up the phone without saying another word. Jim and I are no longer friends.

Code Orange
Fishing

The fish strained left, ran right, jumped, and tried to shake the hook, then darted under the canoe to sulk. It made a last furious run, trying to tunnel its way back to the bottom. Then it was over, and I was proudly hoisting my prize for a quick photograph. Greg, looking through the camera, shook his head and frowned.

"This isn't working for me," he said. "We've got you, a bass, and a couple of guards with M-16s in the background. It looks like you're fishing in a catch-and-release-or-we-shoot zone. Try turning the other way."

I turned, held the bass up, and smiled at the camera again.

"Unh-unh. Those surveillance cameras look like they're growing out of your head. Hang on." He put down the camera, picked up his paddle, and quickly spun the canoe around 180 degrees.

Clearly bored with this process, the bass in question — a solid 4-1/2-pounder with a Rapala Jointed Shad Rap (fire crawdad pattern) hanging from its lip — flapped its tail. It was one of those I-hate-to-intrude-but-I'm-getting-a-little-short-of-breath-here shakes. I unhooked the biggest bass of the summer so far, lowered it back into the water, and watched it dart, unrecorded, back into the depths.

Welcome to Code Orange fishing.

It's not that Greg and I are national security-site junkies. It's just that the bassiest place we know of at the moment is a wall along the Potomac River that borders Fort Lesley McNair, a secure facility that is part of the Military District of Washington and the location of high-value targets like the National Defense University.

In order to access this honey hole by canoe, you launch from behind a green dumpster in back of the U.S. Coast Guard Headquarters, another secure site, which is ringed by concrete barriers. If you smile at the cops as if you do this all the time, they'll generally leave you alone. I don't think they have any specific guidelines for dealing with canoe traffic.

Paddling into position, we were nearly swamped by the wake of the 87-foot cutter

Ibis, which was in the process of anchoring in such a way that its gun covered anything moving in the channel. Two orange-vested cops in a 25-foot inflatable with twin 200-horsepower Yamahas grumbling on the stern idled by and gave us the once-over. As we approached the wall, the pair of guards with M-16s on their shoulders nodded, as if to say, *don't plan on getting back any lures that land on government property.*

The tide was coming in and pushed us steadily up the channel past poles holding hooded surveillance cameras. Pretty soon we were approaching a buoy marking an underground cable, a place that generally holds fish. Just then, one of the guards walked over and announced, "Gentlemen, I'm going to have to ask you to keep at least 30 meters away from that buoy." We said that wouldn't be a problem. He went back to his buddy, and we let the current push us away. Then the other one came over.

"That stuff that guy just told you? I'm going to have to ask you to comply to that right now." We pointed out that the current was accomplishing this fairly quickly. "Yeah, but you're not allowed on this side of the buoy at all. You have to stay at least 30 meters away on the downstream side."

I looked at Greg, who has authority issues

105

under the best of circumstances. "Don't say anything, dummy," I hissed. "I've got to pick up the baby at five, and I can't do it from some damn brig." He put his rod down to pick up a paddle, and we repositioned.

A few minutes later, I caught the big bass. In the next two hours, we boated three more smaller ones and two channel cats — not a bad afternoon's fishing.

"So," Greg said, as we paddled back toward the dumpster-cum-takeout point, "you want to come back Tuesday?"

"Yeah," I said, smiling and waving to a coastguardsman wiping down the gun mounted on the bow of the anchored cutter. "Tuesday's good."

SUMMER SURVIVAL

Things get kind of slow in my neck of the woods around now. Even the bass get bored. Average daily highs in the slow-roast range have pushed the fish into the deepest holes they can find. Slowly finning the coolest water for miles, a pod of big ones watch your lure fall and amuse themselves by competing to be the first to call out the page of the Bass Pro Shops catalog on which it appears. Meanwhile, 20 feet up, we die-hards fish until we're dehydrated, delaminated, and decisively skunked. Back at the dock, we swear on our Power Baits that we will never again go fishing in August. A few days later we're back at it, showing just how severe certain learning disabilities can be.

My summer has been further enhanced by a decision last March to enter the un-official neighborhood lawn contest. That was the month I applied an entire bag of fertilizer (sufficient for 15,000 square feet of grass) to 6,000 square feet of earth. The result is a crop of crabgrass that is growing like hydrilla. If I miss a week with the mower, the Iraqi National Congress could be meeting out back and I wouldn't know it.

I thought I was the only one having a slow summer until I read an Associated Press article about the customers of the Sky Port diner near Schenectady, New York. They recently noticed that Dick, the 17-year-old goldfish in the aquarium behind the counter, was having trouble staying upright. Some people would say, "Well, I'm terribly sorry to hear that, but 17 is really pretty old for a goldfish." Not these folks. They got involved.

One of the regulars prevailed upon his daughter, who is studying to be a veterinarian, to research fish ailments. She decided that Dick's symptoms pointed toward a swim-bladder problem, which she treated by hand-feeding him cooked peas three times a day. Other customers decided that nutritional support was a good first step but no substitute for a comprehensive course of therapy. They got together and built Dick a fish sling so he could recuperate in an upright position. They constructed it out of what any enterprising guy would use: fishing bobbers, soda straws, string, and gauze. Patty Sherman, who co-owns the diner, says customers like to relax at the counter and watch Dick in his homemade sling. Those are the kind of people who understand that the real purpose of summer is not to do very much of anything.

It's hard to imagine when the shingles on your roof are curling in the heat, but bow season starts in less than two months. Every article you've ever read about preparing for it says you must practice shooting in the same clothes you will wear when hunting. This is, of course, ridiculous. I usually hunt in a full Scent-Lok suit, including head cover. Wear that outside on a 95-degree day and you risk two disasters. One is death by heatstroke. The other is ruined hunting gear. The best charcoal-activated suit can absorb only so much body odor over its working life before it throws in the towel.

Nonetheless, I pride myself on having developed an exacting practice routine. I figure that you're probably only going to get one shot at a trophy deer, and it's not going to be when your muscles are warmed up from shooting. So that's how you practice. You march out with a single arrow to a spot in the backyard about 40 yards from your McKenzie deer, draw back, and shoot. If it's a good shot, you go back inside satisfied. If it's a bad shot, you go back inside anyway and mull over what you did wrong for an hour or so, then go shoot another arrow. It's a demanding regimen, but I follow it religiously right up until I miss. Then I say to hell with it, get about eight arrows, and keep shooting until I'm damn sure my target deer no longer presents a threat to anybody in the neighborhood. A rigorous practice routine makes good sense during rigorous times. Summer isn't one of them.

The other day, I had a very close call. At 11 a.m., it was already 97 degrees out, 90 percent humidity, with air quality in the do-not-inhale-before-4 p.m. range. Nonetheless, I always make it a point to be actively engaged in some form of activity before noon — especially when I have nothing in particular to do — so that I can justify knocking off for the day right after lunch. I was busy at my desk when my wife came home unexpectedly and popped in my office door. Instantly, I swept the fishing bobbers, soda straws, string, and gauze into a drawer.

"Whatcha doing?" she asked brightly.

"Oh, you know," I answered, trying to

sound haggard. "Just trying to juggle a million things I've got to get done."

I Want My Bass TV

Nobody was home to stop me last Saturday, so I watched bass shows on cable television for six hours. That's right, six straight hours of rod-bending, line-stretching, heart-pounding action. And when it was all over, I was a new man. I had learned about structure fishing and finesse angling from the experts. I had learned about life on the tournament trail. And every six minutes I had learned about the recent advances in hair replacement and diet supplements that are so important to successful bass fishing.

Perhaps the single most important thing I learned is that, on average, it takes a full 40 hours of raw sewage — sorry, footage — to make a half-hour program. So when the guy on camera finally catches a fish, it unhinges him a little, causing him to repeat what he's saying at least three times. Let me demonstrate with actual quotes (names omitted to protect the guilty):

"Good fish. Nice fish. Healthy fish. And fat. That is one fat fish."

"That's a gorgeous fish. Just a gorgeous, gorgeous fish."

"Oh, man. He just inhaled that spinner-bait. He crushed it. He hammered that thing."

I also learned that there is almost nothing so obvious that you can't say it on bass television. Let me elaborate with more genuine quotes. These are things people actually said. I mean verbally, using their lips:

"If a fish hits your bait right under the boat, you may be too close to the structure. You need to back up."

"If they're not shallow, don't be afraid to look deep."

"Remember, the bass can be in, over, or just off the weed beds. Or any other kind of structure."

"The places where the lines get closer together on your topo maps, those are the places where it's steep. That's where your dropoffs tend to be."

Sometimes the obviousness transcends itself and approaches a kind of bassing epiphany, a Zen moment:

"Those big dudes are in here to feed. And

believe me, if they want it, they'll come get it."

"The Classic is hard to win but very easy to lose."

"You've got to move, move, move. And when you find the fish, they're there."

We'll be right back with more eye-popping action. But first, lean in a little, so I can shout the following question directly into your ear. When is a diet pill worth $153 a bottle? The answer is, When it releases tiny army men directly into your bloodstream to take on fat cells in hand-to-hand combat. Lardbegone is much too expensive and much too powerful for the casual dieter who wants to shed 5 or 10 "vanity" pounds. But if you're so fat that people think you're backing up when your beeper goes off, Lardbegone might be for you.

A number of anglers have expressed concern about what bass fishing is "all about." Fortunately, the experts are only too happy to share their wisdom:

"It all boils down to execution. The final element in your success equation is execution."

"It's all about timing. You might not be here when they're feeding. But if you come back in two hours, you'll catch one every cast. So it's all about timing. And about boat positioning. And banging that cover with your lure. That's what it's all about."

Another thing I noticed is that many television hosts like to kiss the bass they catch. I don't know who started this, but it has become epidemic. And it has to be hurting the catch-and-release survival rate. How strong do you think your will to live would be if the last thing you saw before being set free was an extreme close-up of Woo Daves's lips?

My favorite moment of the whole day came when Babe Winkelman and a friend were banging one largemouth after another on downed timber off a point in a Wisconsin lake.

"Babe," asked the friend, dutifully setting up his host for a sage observation, "does that current going through here have anything to do with why we're catching bass?"

Babe thought on this for a while. Finally, he answered solemnly. "It very well could, Jim."

I can hardly wait for next Saturday.

PARTY ANIMAL

I went to a cocktail party the other night, an activity I don't particularly recommend. For certain men, temporary incarceration in a small space with strangers pretending to have fun ranks right up there with a tax audit. I sometimes doubt that parties would exist at all if it weren't for booze, since the very act of making small talk with people you've never met is so unnatural that you need to be slightly impaired to do it gracefully. But Jane says it's good for me to get out and mingle, so, like a chained bear, several times a year I am dragged out for socialization.

This particular party took place during the height of the pre-rut, and I'd been in the woods until the end of legal light, when I found myself pinned in my tree stand by a doe with two yearlings in tow. Not wanting to burn out the stand by announcing a human presence, I let my bow down on the rope and banged it softly in the leaves a few times. They didn't snort, just stiffened up and moved slowly away. Satisfied, I descended and crept silently out of the darkening woods.

I raced across town to the address Jane had given me, crouched down in the shadows between my car and a hedge, and changed into khakis, a button-down shirt, and loafers. Immediately upon entering, I identified this as a classic disaster-in-the-making: many people, bright lights, the din of forced merriment. Also, I noticed that all the other men not wearing ties had on shirts that buttoned all the way up to the neck. Where I grew up, wearing a shirt buttoned up to the neck without a tie sent out an urgent nonverbal signal: *Please beat me up.* Evidently this has changed, because none of the men seemed the least bit embarrassed by how they were dressed.

I grabbed a beer and saw to my chagrin that Jane was engaged in a lively conversation on the far side of the room. Like many women, my wife finds talking to people she has never met invigorating. I sat down on one end of a sofa and tried hard to make myself invisible. But it didn't work, and I soon found myself face to face with a brightly smiling woman wearing a turquoise necklace. She introduced herself, saying she taught mythology at the local university. "I understand from your wife that you're a writer," she said. "What were you working on today?" I told her that I hadn't been writing at all today, I'd been in the woods hunting deer.

The smile dimmed a few watts, and I could see the wheels turning inside her head. She was having what psychologists call an "Aha!" moment: She'd heard of people who hunted deer, and now she was actually talking to one. "And what do you use," she asked, "some kind of rifle?" I told her that at this time of year I hunted with a bow. This completely flummoxed her. "Like a Robin Hood bow?" she asked. Sort of, I told her. A compound has wheels on it and is a bit more powerful and more compact than Robin Hood's. "Is it electric?" she asked. No, I explained, you pull the string back with your arm just like other bows. I was trying to be helpful, just as she was trying to be cordial, but I was beginning to wish I'd said I was in software.

Just then, she looked away for a moment, pursed her lips, and turned back to me. "I suppose you find it hard to explain why you hunt to people who don't," she said. I do indeed, I told her.

"I read somewhere — I think it was an American Indian elder who said it — that whatever a man hunts, he's ultimately hunting himself," she said. "Is that true? Can you explain that to me?"

I said I thought it was true, though I didn't fully understand it. I told her that for some men, hunting is a kind of discipline, a way of peeling back the layers of mistaken identity that daily life piles up on you. It's a way of discovering who you are, or maybe remembering who you really were before modern life mixed up who you were as a man with what you did to make money. In that sense, at least, every man who hunts is hunting himself. I asked if that made sense.

"Yes," she said. "It makes a lot of sense. Maybe too much." We talked for another couple of minutes before she said she had to go rescue the sitter from her children. She shook my hand and left. I took a pull on my beer and looked around the party. Suddenly I felt looser, a little less scared, like a rabbit who'd been reassured he wasn't to be eaten that particular day. A few minutes later, fetching a second beer, I found myself waiting my turn at the refrigerator next to a guy with mousse in his hair and a dark-green silk number that buttoned up to the neck. "Cool shirt," I said.

THE ART OF LYING

So it's finally over. Either you've got a deer in the freezer or you don't. You're either doing the funky-chicken victory dance or deciding whether to throw your muzzleloader away outright or save it as a tomato stake.

If you did get a deer — and I mean any deer — congratulations. You can sit back and tell the story over and over, until it takes on a life of its own. With each retelling, that deer will get bigger, the shot distance will increase, and the temperature outside will drop a bit more. By about May, you will have killed an animal the size of a moose during a blizzard by blowing a soda-straw wrapper at it from 400 yards. And you will half believe the lies coming out of your own mouth. This is hunting's oldest tradition. In fact, linguists now conjecture that language first arose among hominids to fulfill that most fundamental of impulses: the need to lie. "Korg, this is no bull. I was so close when that mastodon farted that it blew all the hair on my forehead straight back."

Any fool can cope with a punched tag. Venison, a rack to hang in the den — these are child's play. The real test of a hunter's skill is failure. That's when a true sportsman looks into the depths of his soul to see if he can summon up a level of creativity to which a successful hunter can only aspire: It's time to come up with a good excuse. Let's review the options.

(1) Equipment Malfunction

Blaming bad gear is a perennial favorite. Psychologists (most of whom do not hunt) have a pejorative term for this. They call it *blame shifting.* I call it genius. Some samples:

- I drew back on him and there was a rain bubble in my peep. All I could see was an optical illusion of six identical bucks standing side by side, and damned if I didn't shoot the wrong one.
- My scope fogged up. It's like I was hunting in a steam room.
- I was shooting handloads that a buddy swore were the best bullets he'd ever used. And they might be. But when I

121

pulled the trigger, all I heard was *click*.

(2) Tremendous Size of the Animal

Success depends on the hunter seeming every bit as incredulous about the event as the listener.

- You want to know the truth? That buck was so much bigger than I had ever seen around here that I figured it was only 200 yards away. Turns out it was 300 yards off — so I ended up shooting low. All I did was shave a few hairs off his chest. I've got them right here in my wallet. You want to see?

(3) Fear of Collateral Damage

Excuses like this portray you in a favorable light.

- I was just about to pull the trigger on a 10-pointer with a nice drop tine when I noticed a doe right behind him. I just couldn't bring myself to take the shot.

(4) Too Wild to Be Contradicted

You need to say something so outrageous that your listener must either accept it at face value or call your bluff. This works best with guys who are smaller than you. Assume a somewhat belligerent tone, as if you're tired of explaining the obvious.

- That bullet hit a gravity sump. Oh, yeah, they're all over the place. See, gravity acts a lot like a liquid. You didn't know that? Yeah, and there are spots where the force of gravity pools up and concentrates. You can't map them because they migrate. I could shoot over one and it would just about eat my bullet up — drop it like a stone halfway to a deer. Next day, that sump would have moved on. You could shoot there and everything would be fine.

(5) Verbal Jujitsu

Use your listener's own momentum against him in a way he doesn't expect, causing him to fly out the window. Look to the left and right when he asks how you failed to get your deer, as if making sure nobody else can eavesdrop on the profound secret you're about to reveal. Take a step closer to the person and motion for him to bend in toward you. Take another look around, lean in toward his ear, and whisper so softly that even he will not be sure you actually had the audacity to say the following:

- I missed.

The truth, used sparingly, can be the most astounding excuse of all.

WATER TORTURE

I have absolutely no business being here. None of us do. But on an unseasonably warm spring day like this one, when the sun decides to punch in for work for the first time in five months, it happens. You head out on some fool household errand and the next thing you know your car has driven you down to the river. And there, standing around the boathouse parking lot like convicts counting the days until their release, are half a dozen guys just like you. We are wearing pinstriped suits and plumber's coveralls, leaning against waxed Suburbans and rusted panel trucks. And to a man we are tantalized and transfixed by that water sliding away just out of reach.

It's too soon. It's still winter, season of extra layers, road salt, and despair. The water is too high, too muddy, and too cold. The first decent chance you have of something hitting a hook is two weeks away,

125

minimum. We know this. We know it's spring doing her annual striptease, that the universe is just yanking our chains. It's just that we're fishermen and we can't help ourselves. So we've come to stare at the water as if we can speed up spring by telepathy.

Here's the drill where I live. The first perch don't even think about migrating up the river until the water temperature hits 47, and they don't start biting in earnest until it's in the low to mid-50s. Then come the other migratory fish, the shad and herring. Only after that do the bass, crappie, and catfish turn on.

It would be easier all around if fish lived in the air. Air's a pushover. You throw it a little sunlight and it snuggles into your arms and coos, *My place or yours?* Even soil heats up fairly fast. A single warm day like this one has no problem coaxing the daffodils and forsythia into promiscuous behavior they'll regret with tomorrow's cold snap. But water remembers what Mama told her. She requires the prolonged application of warmth before she comes around.

Danny, who has worked at the boathouse all his life, is busy with the annual repainting of the rowboats. Today he's got three up on sawhorses, like giant turtles stranded on their backs in the sun. They're 141/2 feet long and made of white oak. Some are 60 years old. They've been painted the same colors for as long as anyone can remember: brick red to the waterline, battleship gray beneath.

"The color never changes, only what they call it," Danny says. "Most years it's been 'tile' or 'brick,' sometimes 'burnt brick.' But lately they've been going a little overboard. Guess the marketing guys have to earn their pay. Last year it was 'Hessian.' "

"What the heck is a Hessian?" I ask.

"I was wondering that, too. So I looked it up. It's a German mercenary serving in the British forces during the American Revolution."

I guess Danny's got too much time on his hands, too. I ask what the color is this year.

" 'Matador,' " he says.

"No. Come on."

He gestures to the can, and I bend over to look. Sure enough, matador. So now we're waiting for the water to get warm enough for the running of the bulls. Fine. Whatever. Just hurry it up.

By now, most of the stranded anglers have drifted over to watch Danny. We envy him. At least he's got something to do with his hands. The group watches silently as a fat

127

honeybee sets down on a section he has just painted.

"The color," he murmurs to no one in particular. "They think it's a flower." There is not much to be done about a honeybee who tries to suck nectar from a red rowboat, just as there isn't much to be done about an angler who tries to pull fish from a too-cold river. Danny turns to load his brush, and when he looks back the bee is gone.

"Oh, good," he says. "She got away."

The phone rings and he answers it. " 'Bout two weeks," he says. "But keep checking with us because you never know when they'll start moving." He listens for a moment. "Look, I could give you dates. I try to predict it every year, and I've never been right yet." He listens again, making a circular motion with his free hand to indicate that the guy just doesn't get it. Finally he sighs and says, "Sure, you can go fishing now. You just have to lower your expectations. Heck, I'm standing here with six guys. And every one of us is dying to go fishing."

To a man, we smile ruefully, shove our hands that much deeper into our pockets, and stare out at the water.

STALKING
WALT DISNEY

It all began innocently enough. Okay, maybe not so innocently.

It was Sunday. My wife had just headed off to hunt the malls. The deal we have is that Jane takes care of Emma, our 3-1/2-year-old, when I hunt. And vice versa (Latin for "clean up the kitchen, too") when she goes out. In short, I was looking at six hours of solo baby duty. I scanned the house for resources and found the usual suspects: videocassettes manufactured by the Walt Disney Corp. or its imitators, each of which Emma has seen 9,000 times.

One of her current favorites is *Spirit: Stallion of the Cimarron,* in which a "wild" horse declares his kinship to all living things, asserting that his kind had always belonged in the West and always would. The horses in *Spirit* speak only in voice-overs, but they have enormous eyebrows to mime their moral outrage at the white men who are building railroads through their lands. They have a burning desire — not like real horses, which want merely to eat, sleep, and avoid feeding their foals to coyotes — to run free, "like the wind in the buffalo grass."

There is also *The Fox and the Hound,* in which all the animals of the forest — carnivores included — live in a kind of vegetarian paradise until unseen hunters orphan an adorable little fox named Todd. The one hunter who does appear in the movie has a big mustache made entirely of nose hair. At one point, we see him approach a posted fence that reads, NO HUNTING, GAME PRESERVE. His eyes narrow. "Well, now, we ain't gonna do none o' that, are we, Copper?" he says sweetly to his dog. "We're just gonna get us a no-good fox!"

It suddenly struck me that Emma's hunting soul was in mortal danger. And that the only thing necessary for the triumph of evil in this world is for enough good men to allow Walt Disney to explain the outdoors to their children.

"Monkey!" I cried, "this is your lucky day. We're going hunting!" Emma didn't know what the words meant, but she liked my enthusiasm. I checked the short-term survival kit: diapers, wipes, juice boxes, and cheese sticks. I strapped her in the baby seat. Off we roared to some deer woods I'd been meaning to scout.

"Where going?" Emma asked at one point.

"Hunting!" I said.

"Hunting!" Emma echoed.

We were actually only going scouting, of course. But I didn't want to confuse her with details. These particular woods were loaded with sign: old rubs and scrapes, fresh droppings, loads of trails.

"Emma!" I said. "Pay dirt! There are deer everywhere here!" We started down a tunnel-like trail. Emma, at just under 30 pounds and just over 30 inches tall, is built for this. She sprinted down the tunnels, delighted at my inability to keep up. At a place where two trails crossed, I explained that this was a good spot to put a tree stand, so you could ambush the deer with a bow and arrow.

"Like yours?" she asked. Sure, I replied, only we'd have to get her a smaller bow and little arrows. She beamed. "Little arrows for me!"

We followed tracks. We practiced sneaking through the woods. Every so often, I would pretend to spot a deer running away and lift Emma up to look at it. She always saw it. Then she started seeing her own imaginary deer and pointing them out to me just as

131

they faded into nothingness. Long story short, we had a blast. Best of all, she was hooked on hunting without seeing anything more than deer sign.

Three hours later, when Mom came home, Emma and I were glued to a different kind of video: *Whitetail Madness 5,* featuring 13 hunts with bow and gun. Emma was transfixed. "Here comes the buck," she whispered as a big 12-pointer lumbered into range. I'd already gone online and ordered a Genesis bow, a wonderful invention that accommodates draw lengths from 15 to 30 inches and that can have its draw weight adjusted to as low as 10 pounds.

"Mommy, c'mere!" Emma squealed. "Watch 'em get this buck!"

Jane dropped her packages on the kitchen counter and sighed. She is from a nonhunting background, and while she has struggled to understand my passion for deer, she would just as soon not have the other preschool moms know that I am creating a shameless outdoorswoman.

"Mommy!" Emma called again. "They got him! Dubba lung shot! Whoo-ooh!"

Jane exited the room, shaking her head. "Watch it again?" Emma suggested, grinning.

"You bet," I said, and we high-fived.

"Daddy?" she asked a minute later. "Take this movie to school for show-and-tell?"

I could see it now: outraged phone calls from the Volvo moms, an emergency PTA meeting, a resolution that I not be allowed within 500 feet of preschool.

"Maybe not," I told Emma. I put my head next to hers and whispered, "But I like your spirit, Monkey. You and me, we're hunters."

"Oooh," she said, lost in the video. "Here comes the buck."

2004: A Huntin' Odyssey

The time has come to admit that traditional hunting no longer fits the lifestyle of the modern recreator. Why? First, because it occurs outdoors. No place is more subject to rapid and uncomfortable changes in temperature. Nowhere are you more likely to encounter as many snakes, ticks, or harmful bacteria.

Second — a major inconvenience — in traditional hunting you are not the one who determines when you hunt. A bunch of illiterate quadrupeds are in charge of scheduling. So you rise in the middle of the night, put on badly tailored orange clothing, and head out. Then, just to make it really fun, you hike until you're hypothermic (elk), squint through powerful optics until you have a headache (mule deer), or sit motionless in a tree stand until a brown recluse spider builds a web in your ear (whitetails). And while you sit there like some fluorescent Buddha — unable even to scratch your butt, much less use your cell phone — your wallet is very active. It is hemorrhaging money, gushing an endless stream of cash for gear, licenses, leases, vehicles, and the beer you require to numb the pain after you have finished for the day and have nothing to show for it.

To sum up traditional hunting: tedium, discomfort, and the loss of disposable income. If this is really what you're after, try matrimony. But we live in an age of miracles. The technology and entertainment industries have come to our rescue with a new and better way to hunt. All a person needs is a personal computer: Fire it up, slap in a disc, and go virtual huntin'.

The preview opens with pristine mountains, a tranquil lake, and, in the distance, a monumental brown bear gorging on blueberries. Up comes the pounding rock music that hunting has lacked until now, and the screen turns into crosshairs. Then comes the crack of a rifle and — whoa! — suddenly you're riding the bullet cam, the landscape streaking by before the round slams into the shoulder of the grizzly. The bear drops like a cement truck. Sweet. HEART SHOT! reads the screen as celebratory fireworks explode. The game takes a photo of the hunter and bear. Then it drags the already taxidermied animal to a pedestal in the trophy room of a log cabin. Awesome.

Now it's my turn. So many choices. I select elk from the game-animal menu, and Montana for a location. But first, a quick stop by the weapons locker for, oh, maybe a .338 Winchester Mag. Sure, it's a lot of gun. But virtual recoil is real easy on the shoulder. I take a moment to familiarize myself with the controls. I particularly like the "strafe left" and "strafe right" functions. And there are three gauges at the bottom of the screen, indicating my strength, level of fitness, and . . . what looks like oil pressure. Whatever. I'm not a detail guy.

The computer loads the geometry, geography, and artificial intelligence — very cutting edge. Next thing I know, I'm at the little hunting shack in Montana I will never own. There is an ATV idling a few feet away. I hop on and roar away. But I keep hitting rocks and trees. Then I fall off, sustain a broken arm, and have to start over. This time I hike to the top of a small mountain and do some glassing. There's lots of nice scenery but no elk. Then I accidentally right-click the mouse and discharge my weapon. The game voice says, "I don't think so." Even sarcasm is built in.

On the third try I discover a really cool thing: When I hit a river, I do a breaststroke right through it and don't even get wet. But then the opposite bank is so steep I can't climb out. I flail around for a while until I drown, sinking slowly into the murky blue depths. Bummer. Back to start.

Okay, no more ATV, no more swimming. Now I hunt smart. I walk for about six days and finally see a herd of elk in the distance. There is a bull with antlers the size of telephone poles. I drop to a prone position and am sneaking into range when a tremor in my finger accidentally clicks the mouse and I blow off my virtual kneecap. My oil pressure drops to nothing, my computer emits a warning that does not sound like part of the game, and the screen turns bright blue. Then an error message appears: *This program has performed an illegal operation and cannot be restarted.*

Defeated, I glance outside. The scenery is all incredibly realistic: the yellow leaves, the cracked bark on the trees, the soft whoosh of the wind. Suddenly, an electrical impulse runs through my cranial hardware: I could actually try hunting outdoors. The idea is so far outside the box that some might call it crazy. But like many gamers, I'm a wild man at heart.

THE BOOK OF JOHN

Around this time each year a loud thump outside the house announces to millions of American sportsmen that the new Cabela's catalog has just hit the front porch, flattening any flowerpot, bicycle, or dog on which it lands. After burying Duke in the vegetable patch, the breathless recipients attach a heavy chain from their ATV to the document and drag it into the bathroom for a first look. This lasts, on average, half an hour. Then, a simultaneous flushing of toilets causes reservoirs nationwide to fall 6 inches, injuring thousands of Jet Skiers and proving once again the existence of a just and loving God.

The word *catalog* comes from the Greek *katalogos,* literally "words causing income to vanish." But *catalog* hardly begins to describe this magical work. A quick perusal yields information to live by. For instance, raise your hand if you knew any of the following three facts:

- A box of Weatherby Magnum Ultra-Velocity ammo in .30/378 Weatherby Mag., 200-grain Nosler Partition, will run you $90, or about $4.50 per shell. At that price, you might want to let that Cape buffalo get really close before wasting a shot.
- For about 50 bucks more you can get a pair of Cabela's Kangaroo Upland Bird Boots, which weigh almost nothing, are a whopping 62 percent stronger than cowhide, and will still be going strong when you are pushing up chokecherry. Of course, state law prohibits their shipment to California for fear of offending celebrity animal rights activists.
- Nothing screams "good taste" to your houseguests like a $60 clear-acrylic toilet seat in which fishing lures, bullets, or hooks are embedded.

The most recent catalog runs to 711 pages and weighs more than some Korean automobiles. The day is coming when a cabela will refer to a unit of weight. You will buy crushed stone and pig iron by the cabela. Diet pills will promise to help you shed those unwanted cabelas. Olympic lifters will bow their heads in silent tribute to the brave Ukrainian champion who was crushed when he attempted to clean and jerk what would have been a new world record of 100 cabelas.

Dick Cabela's empire started out small. Back in 1961, he placed a three-line ad in a magazine offering five hand-tied flies to any customer who would cover the 25-cent postage. Orders were processed at the company headquarters, Dick's kitchen table in Chapell, Nebraska. The flies were sent back with a mimeographed sheet listing other sporting items for purchase. The operation has been so successful that nearly 6,000 employees now work in that kitchen. Mary, Dick's wife, is said to be tired of having to make them sandwiches every day and thinks it's about time to build a cafeteria.

The Cabela's catalog has long exercised a strange power over otherwise rational men. As you consider it in the privacy of the best seat in the house, it starts to seem like a good idea — no, a responsibility — to buy not only what you need immediately but also gear that you *might need some day.* Thus, guys who live on fishing boats in Alaska suddenly crave 17-inch camo snake boots. Others who have difficulty opening the hood of their truck covet the titanium-handled Leatherman Charge XTi with nine double-end bits should they ever run out of gas in the wilderness and have to drill for oil. Guys who've never bushwhacked through cover worse than the azaleas in their front yard must have the Filson Double Tin Cloth Chaps that stop the smaller shotgun loads at close range.

I recently ordered the handheld Thor 10-million-candle-power spotlight. Why? Because let me ask you something: How stupid are you going to feel when hordes of eye-sucking aliens invade Earth and your entire family dies just because you lacked the wattage to signal other planets for help?

My personal weakness is footwear. I'm the kind of guy who can't be happy if my feet aren't. That's why I need the Trans-Alaska III pacs endorsed by the winner of the Iditarod and rated to minus 135 degrees. Overkill? We'll see who's laughing when the next ice age hits. And I know the chances that the editors of this magazine will call to say "Heavey! Next plane to Alaska. Bighorn sheep" are slim. But slim is not none. That's why I need the $270 boots handcrafted by Austrian elves and featuring the Vibram multigrip outsole and removable Air-Active footbeds designed for precisely that kind of hunting.

I could go on. I'd like to. But my daughter is banging on the bathroom door and calling me a doo-doo head. Don't forget the camo bedding on page 327. The Mossy Oak Shadow Grass window treatments are particularly spiffy. And now, Jet Skiers of America, say your prayers.

■ ■ ■ ■

III
THE JUNKET JACKPOT:
HUNTING AND FISHING
AS "WORK"

■ ■ ■ ■

THE LION DOGS

The dogs are free-casting along a wash at the bottom of a nameless canyon in the Atacosa Mountains a few miles north of the Mexican border, silently nosing for lion scent, when all eight blow up. The almost mournful hysteria of the pack echoes off the canyon walls, bypasses the rational brain, and reaches into something deeper, some preverbal place where the laws of men no longer obtain. All at once there is a coppery taste in my mouth, blood hammering into my ears, and I'm alive in a way I wasn't just a moment ago. Barely an hour into the first day of the hunt, it looks as if we may get ludicrously lucky on the most elusive predator in North America.

My guide, Jonathon Kibler, dismounts his mule to look for a print. So does Wally Kostelnik, another guide who is helping Kibler on this trip and has brought some of his dogs along, too. Unlike most other North

American game, mountain lions leave what is known as "heavy" scent, evaporating so slowly that the dogs can't tell which way the track heads. In the quickly vanishing art of bare-ground hunting — all Kibler does and just about all he cares about — you must hunt for a print or other sign lest you track the animal backward.

A few minutes later, Kibler draws a circle in the gravel with his boot heel and motions me over. With my nose inches from the ground, I finally make out what he has seen from his mount: the four toes and two ridges left by the clefts in the heel lobe, which, taken together, spell lion. Lion tracks are hard to see. One reason is that dirt is scarce in this part of Arizona, and any terrain not covered by rock is covered by thorns. Another is that a cougar puts its feet straight down instead of rolling them, so no debris is thrown behind the track. And since a cougar extends its claws only when killing or fighting, it leaves no scratch marks. This track is just a few hours old. The dogs are headed the right way. From the frenzied note in their bawling, Kibler thinks the lion is very close. "We just may catch this one," he says. Photographer Dusan Smetana jumps down to get a shot of the print in the morning light, then trots his mule fast to catch up with the three of us.

Perfect Predators

Truth is, I'm not sure I want to shoot a mountain lion. Maybe it's professional courtesy. We're both hunters, after all, and the lion outranks me in every aspect of the game except abstract reasoning. It has the widest distribution of any native mammal in the Western Hemisphere, from northern British Columbia to the Strait of Magellan. An adult tom averages 140 pounds and can bring down a 1,000-pound elk, antlers and all. When it kills, it fastens its jaws to the back of the prey's neck, snapping it by twisting the head with a blow from its paw. A lion can pounce 20 feet or more from a standstill. Lions have been observed dropping 65 feet from a tree to the ground without injuring themselves. This is partly because a mountain lion's entire dismantled skeleton would fit inside a hiking boot box. The creature is all muscle and sinew.

My motivations are further complicated by the fact that I've always thought you had a responsibility to eat what you kill. Although you can eat lion (it's pink and tastes a little like pork, which, of course, is exactly the way cannibals describe human flesh), I'm not after meat. Like most hunters, I've heard about lions most of my life and have seen exactly zero of them in the wild. To me, they are the embodiment of stealth, secrecy, and skill. And now that we've struck a trail, I'm obsessed with encountering one face-to-face.

Of course, this is only the first day. I harbor no ambivalence about the chase. I can't wait to hunt the animal, to see where it lives and how it moves when trying to elude the dogs. I'll trust my gut on whether to shoot. That moment will come if and when we've bayed the lion and Kibler asks if I want his Ruger .44 Magnum, the one with the 11-inch barrel he keeps in a special leather holster a friend made for him that bears a line of scripture incised on the inside of the flap. I've been nailing orange-juice jugs with the pistol back at camp. Kibler has it sighted in at 100 yards with 240-grain solid points. Most shots on bayed lions are at distances of less than 15 yards.

The dogs boil up the wash, then veer off to follow the scent trail straight up the steep side of the canyon into red rock bluffs and then along the canyon ridge. The trail leads into even higher bluffs, follows the spine of the ridge farther, and then drops back into the canyon. Going up was scary; going down you distract yourself by composing potential epitaphs because you can see exactly where you'll end up if your mule slips. (At the moment, I'm thinking I TOLD YOU IT WAS A LITTLE TOO STEEP might be appropriate. Kibler uses mules because they're stronger and more sure-footed than horses. "When a horse loses its footing, it starts scrambling, just like humans do. A mule will just drop down onto its brisket, put its feet back under itself, and get up." Equally important, mules won't spook at the scent of lions or blood.) I'm leaning so far back in the saddle that my head nearly rests on the hindquarters of the mule I've christened Tylenol in honor of the medication I will be doubling up on should I make it back to camp in one piece. The cougar crosses its track once, then again, and now, three hours later, we are almost back where we picked up the scent.

Suddenly the dogs go quiet. "I'll be damned." Kibler pushes his new gray Stetson, the exact color of his mustache, back on his head, looks up into the bluffs, and lets out a long breath. "Tell you exactly what happened," he elaborates at last. "That cat watched us walk 100 yards below him two hours ago, waited until we'd passed, and took off." When a lion is hunting or alarmed, he explains, it reflexively shuts down its scent, which is why the dogs can no longer pick up a trail. Biologists haven't proved this yet, but it has long been axiomatic among experienced lion men. In any case, this lion has too much of a head start and is no longer leaving enough scent to follow. "That's about as close to catching one as you can get and not do it," he says.

The Lost Art

It's not enough to be good when you're chasing lions over bare ground. You also need to be lucky. That's why Kibler's hunts last 10 days. So many things affect the dogs' ability to scent — humidity, temperature, sunlight, how long it's been since it rained, even the wind — that it may not be worthwhile to loose the dogs some days. But if you get on lions (and Kibler usually does get on five or six in that time), eventually you will probably guess right and catch one. If you last that long. "I've had hunters go out, spend 10 hours like we did today, and ask to be taken straight to the airport that same night," he says with a grin. "A lot of guys don't like to do this because it's so hard."

As for me, I'm already hooked — on the bawling of the dogs, the beauty and scale of the country, the clop of mule hooves against stone, and the possibility that this may be the day you catch an animal most hunters go their whole lives without seeing. Maybe most of all, I'm hooked on the aesthetics of this kind of hunting. Some things are supposed to be hard. The difficulty is precisely what makes them matter so much.

Fifty years ago, there were hundreds of guys in the Southwest like Jon Kibler, who carried between their ears centuries of accumulated knowledge. Now there are a few dozen. In a generation or so, the only bareground lion hunters left will likely be made of wax and paint in museum dioramas. Not so long ago most ranchers kept a pack of dogs to deal with the mountain lions that preyed on their livestock. The dogs were bred and taught to hunt close to their owners, to ignore all game other than what they were trained to hunt, and, once on the scent, to follow it until they dropped from exhaustion or their master called them off. The body of knowledge that grew up around training lion dogs and hunting big cats wasn't written down because nobody thought it needed to be. You couldn't learn it from a book anyway. You had to go out and do it.

Wave bye-bye to those days and those men, because you won't be seeing them again. Today's "rancher" is an absentee landlord who leases the land to someone who has no proprietary interest in keeping it up. New roads make it easy to get into what was once remote lion country. Today's cowboy saddles up a four-wheel-drive truck, an ATV, and a snowmobile to get where he wants to go. Radio collars mean it's no longer necessary to spend the hours it takes to train dogs to hunt close. Cell phones allow groups of widely separated hunters all after the same lion to coordinate their movements. And Kibler, 56 — who wears spurs first worn by his grandfather, was born on a farm, and has been raising and training his own dogs for more than 30 years — is fully aware that he is one of the last of his kind, a dinosaur. He's even thinking of trying to write a book about what he knows, not so much to teach as to document what once was common knowledge. He wants to call it *The Lost Art.*

Tough Dogs

Over steaks, double margaritas, and lots of Tylenol back at the trailer that serves as camp, I ask Kibler about which breeds work best on lions. "Now you're opening a Pandora's box," he says. "See, I'm not stuck on breeds. I'm stuck on something else entirely:

ability." He explains that for a lion dog in the Southwest, it starts with good feet. It takes three to four years to get a dog up to snuff, and in the country he hunts, a dog will be lame by then unless it has tough feet. That the dog needs a good cold nose goes without saying. Beyond that it has to have the determination to stay on a scent trail for 8 or 10 hours without flagging. This is known as the ability to "pound" or "hammer" the track. But a dog also must be able to run the lion fast enough to force it into a bluff or up a tree — to "drive" or "push" the track. Bitter experience has taught him that registered hounds rarely fit the bill. Walkers, for instance, don't have the foot toughness or the desire to keep pounding, although they are fast on a jump race after the lion has been sighted. Plotts don't have enough nose, and the 30 or so Kibler has owned over the years were weak in homing instinct. A dog that can't find its way back to the truck won't make it in this country. Blueticks, though blessed with good cold noses and toughness, are hardheaded and won't push as hard as required. Redbones are good coon dogs, but he finds they lack the determination and drive for bigger game. Black-and-tans are ideal in many ways. They have good noses, will pound a track all day, and have tons of determination. The only problem is that they're black, which is the wrong color for the Southwest. They tend to overheat. Kibler finds that the best dog for lions where he hunts is a combination of Walker, black-and-tan, and bluetick. Such a dog comes in a variety of colors, depending on its genetic makeup. His are a rainbow coalition bound together by a desire to hunt so strong that the ones left behind on a given day sometimes manage to break their chains and follow.

"I've been lucky," he says. "Never lost a dog lion hunting. I've had them torn up pretty bad by lions — had them fall, get snakebit, and go lost for days. And I did lose a sweet dog, Annie, many years ago when she overheated one day. She died about 45 minutes before we got to the water that probably would have saved her. That was tough. But all in all, I've been real lucky." Wally Kostelnik says that in 12 years, he has had to put down one dog that got bit through the head by a lion. Both men count themselves unusually fortunate. They say that dogs' falling off bluffs is an ever present danger. Lions bay up in high places, and the hounds follow. What happens is that a bunch will get to jostling one another trying to get at the cat, and the one closest to the edge goes over. Fortunately, neither man's dogs have ever had a long fall.

Kibler himself nearly got killed once out here. It was five years ago, when a young mule he was training started bucking on a steep descent. The mule went down and landed on him. He sustained a concussion, dislocated his left shoulder, fractured his left shoulder blade, fractured two ribs in front, tore three ribs out of his spine, and dislocated his right hip. "I woke up after about half an hour or so, looked at the client I'd been guiding for the better part of a week, and asked, 'Who're you?' " The doctors told him he'd also twisted his vertebrae the same way that left Christopher Reeve paralyzed from the neck down, only Kibler had so much muscle in his neck that it had kept his spinal column from being severed. "I was laid up awful bad. The doc said he thought he could get me to where I'd walk again, but that I'd never ride or hunt." Kibler didn't even bother arguing. After obeying orders for 10 months, one day he got back in the saddle and resumed chasing lions.

An Unforgiving Land
The next day, we make a 20-mile loop that starts at sunup and ends about 3 o'clock.

During this time Kibler admires my Filson Tin Cloth jacket ("That's the stuff to have out here. I go through a Carhartt a year") and tells me the names of the plants that are drawing blood from the unprotected parts of my body: ocotillo, which has spiny tendrils 10 to 12 feet long, shin dagger, cat-claw acacia (also known locally as "wait-a-minute"), and, worst of all, a subspecies of cholla cactus called Teddy Bear, whose dense spines will break off and cling to you if you brush against them. The dogs are silent the whole day. When a panicked jackrabbit zigzags right through the pack, they don't even break stride. When we finally get back to a cold beer and a seat without a pommel or stirrups, Kibler looks strangely satisfied. "You know, a guy who didn't know dogs would come in from a day like that and think it was a failure," he says. "But look at it this way. We were crossing deer, bobcat, javelina, rabbit, and illegal alien tracks all day. And you saw how those dogs never broke off. That's discipline. That's dogs who know their business." Lying on my sleeping bag, feeling as if I've been beaten by invisible elves with ball peen hammers, I find myself wondering exactly how far away the nearest codeine is and whether the dogs could be trained to find it for me.

On the final day of the hunt, we ride into a place called Hell's Gate, where several canyons come together. Almost immediately, the dogs strike in the dry creek bed. Kibler finds a print showing that the lion is headed the opposite way and gets the dogs turned around and headed back up Peck Canyon. But the scent peters out atop a tower of rock in the creek bed. "I'm thinking this is old scent, by the way the dogs are acting," he says. "That cat might have laid up here for the night. Let's keep going the way we were headed and see what happens." Twenty minutes later, the dogs strike again, and even I can tell it's a hot track. There is something in their voices that brings back the copper taste and the blood pounding in my ears. Kibler wants me to inspect the print he has found, but I can't make it out from the saddle and don't want to waste time trying with the dogs howling so hysterically. He thinks it's a female or a young tom. We follow for a couple of miles, the dogs working steadily up and down the scent trail. It breaks left and up toward the red bluffs. The dogs scamper straight up, but the mules have to zigzag their way, setting off small rockslides at each turn.

My fear of falling is still with me. But now I realize that the mule has greater balance, strength, and a more even disposition than I do. So I'm probably safer on him than on foot. I just want him to walk faster so that we can catch the lion. Sore muscles and all, I'm feeling strangely privileged to be alive and in this place at this moment. Right now — with the sun warming my back, little wildflowers poking their heads up from between the rocks, and the ancient music of the hounds floating on the air — I'm convinced there could be no more vivid or glorious way to spend your life than chasing lions.

As we near the base of the bluffs, we see the dogs spread out in a line racing along the rim of the canyon above us. They reach the saddle, cross it, and keep running up along the even higher ridge on the far side. Then they cross out of sight, just over the top and into Beehive Canyon. We try two routes that dead-end into walls before we find one where we can lead the mules up a narrow opening, bearing up to the ridge and across the saddle. Kostelnik thinks he hears the dogs faintly from Beehive, and it sounds as though they've got the lion bayed.

Half an hour later we finally arrive at the base of the tall red rock bluffs that make up the far ridge. These are higher and steeper than any we've been on. We tie the mules. The dogs are up top, just out of view but barking loudly and nonstop. "Climb," Kibler orders. "Fast." He takes off ahead of me. Kostelnik is headed up a different route, just to our left, with Smetana and his cameras at his heels. It's all-fours work, like climbing the Great Pyramid, scaling one big boulder to another, crashing through thorny undergrowth that tears at your clothes.

When we crest the bluffs, the wind is blowing hard and dogs are boiling all over the place as they try to get to the cat, which is hidden in the rocks a few yards below us. It's a long way down to Peck Canyon, the one we've just come from. It's an even longer drop into Beehive, in front of us. There are some places where you could climb down into Beehive, others where you'd just fall. "Right here!" roars Kostelnik, who is standing below us on a ledge and pointing to a place directly below me and out of my sight. Smetana is with him, already down on one knee and shooting film. I hear the lion hiss but can't see it. I start to make my way left and down to the narrow ledge where the two men are, but something makes me stop and size up the situation. It's only 10 feet from me to their ledge, but there are no decent handholds between here and there. The dogs are scrambling all over the rock in a frenzy to get at the cat, and I know I'm too excited to be jumping around up here. Then I look down and realize that I can't see the bottom; I've reached a sort of chute in the bluffs. One slip here and your life ends. I drop to all fours as a trembling brown dog scrambles over me as though I'm just another piece of rock. By sheer force of will, the dog manages to cling to the rocks on the path I've just decided I won't be taking. It attains the ledge and immediately charges ahead for the lion. The mad barking of the dogs has somehow risen to an even more frenzied pitch. I reverse direction and head up a few feet, trying to find another way down. Back where I was a long minute ago, I'm still just above the lion but unable to see it. Again the cat hisses. It's not loud. The lion knows the dogs are more nuisance than threat. But a lion won't stay bayed forever. Sooner or later it will decide to take off.

I look over the edge again, on the off chance that the cat may have moved to where I can at least glimpse it. Just at that moment, I hear the men below both shouting at the same time. Then I watch, horrified, as two dogs fall off the ledge below me. They wriggle silently in the air, spinning their back legs for something, anything, to push against. The next moment they're gone. "Two dogs gone," I call to Kibler somewhere above me, trying to keep control over my voice. I hear Kostelnik shouting some more, and this time he's cursing. The lion made her move moments before, bounding right between Kostelnik and Smetana and leaping from ledge to ledge, then vanishing over a ridge. Either she swatted the dogs over or they were jostled. But the toll is not yet complete. A third dog has also fallen to its death. Then Kibler, whom I've not seen all this time, though he has been just above me, yells that another dog went over, too, but apparently landed 30 feet down on a ledge. For the moment, that one is presumed alive. The dogs are still barking like crazy, but suddenly everything has changed. This is the dark side of that ancient music, the price that can be exacted at any time when men and dogs and wild game get mixed up together.

Kibler, Smetana, and I meet atop the rocks. "We're not hunting lions anymore today," Kibler says evenly. "We're hunting dogs." It takes us a while to get the remaining hounds leashed. All three of the lost —

Tilly, Sally, and Spook — belong, by pure happenstance, to Kostelnik. Brownie, the one that fell onto the ledge below, is Kibler's. Kostelnik has already gone, taking the long way down to the canyon floor to find the bodies of his dogs and retrieve their collars. Kibler and I gather the remaining five dogs — we took off with nine today — and take them down to where we've tied the mules. Kibler is all business. "I really need you to stay here and keep these dogs quiet," he tells me, his face just inches from mine so I'll understand exactly what he's saying. "If they start barking, smack 'em. Hard. Use a stick if you have to. I'm afraid Brownie might do something stupid and fall if she hears them." He retrieves the 30 feet of cotton rope he carries in his saddlebags, undoes one of the mules' leads to add to it, and disappears at full speed back up the rocks. I sit with the mules and the straining dogs for 45 minutes, clamping a hand over their muzzles whenever they howl. I try to stop replaying the image of the dogs in free fall. I'm okay, I can think clearly, but I'm not all right.

Finally Kibler and Smetana come back with Brownie on a leash. Kibler is wearing a tight smile, a mixture of regret and joy, and shaking his head. "You're looking at the luckiest dog in the world right now." He tells how he put a loop in the end of the rope and dropped it down to the ledge. Miraculously, it caught on the one tiny bush down there. Miraculously, it landed with the loop open. When he called Brownie, she turned toward his voice and — miraculously — stuck her neck and one leg into the loop. He jerked the rope closed and hauled her to safety. Her rescue, like Kostelnik's loss of three dogs in an instant, is a 1-in-1,000 shot. Yet both have come to pass in the same hour.

Kostelnik finally returns with three collars in hand and slumps heavily against a rock. He is a big guy, a weight lifter and lifelong outdoorsman who works as a firefighter in Phoenix when he's not guiding. He doesn't want to talk, doesn't want his sandwich, doesn't want to be consoled. "They were the heart of my pack, some of my best dogs" is all he'll say. "You couldn't have bought those dogs off me for $10,000." There is a force field of grief around him, and nothing to do but mount up and start the long ride back to camp.

After the Fall

During dinner we make small talk about everything but the elephant standing in the corner, the lost dogs. I've endured enough losses in my life to learn that silence is the worst remedy for grief. Suddenly, my eyes are wet, and everyone's busy not looking at me. "Jesus, Wally, they weren't even my dogs and I'm all broke up about them," I say. "It must be worse for you." He clamps a big hand on my shoulder for a second, then goes back to scraping a frying pan clean. But at least the elephant is gone now. The grief has been spoken. A little while later, he starts talking about Sally, who was his best dog, a superb striker, a dog that never walked over a track and would push it harder than any other dog he ever saw. Kibler recalls Annie, the dog he lost to heatstroke a few years back. "I've been raising dogs for more than 40 years now, and you never get over the ones that die before their time."

The next day we pack up. Kostelnik loads his mules and dogs into his truck. Then he goes to perform his last chore, fetching the three chains and water bowls that no longer belong to any dog. Our good-byes are formal. His suffering still hangs about him like a parka.

As I'm driving out, Kibler, walking to his truck, smiles and gives me a wink. It is a throwaway gesture that somehow contains a lifetime's worth of experience and wisdom. It's as if he's acknowledging that, sure, we had some hard luck. But you can't give up because of that. Despair is a bigger liar than hope will ever be. Broken hearts are made whole again in time. The gesture stays with me for a long drive and two plane rides, until I'm finally home.

A week later, Kibler calls me. "I wanted to let you know Wally's okay. He took it hard, but he's hunting again. He found out the sun still comes up and the world still turns, so he figured he'd better get his pack back in shape. There's still a lot of lions to be caught down here."

We make small talk for a while. Then we get down to business. I ask when exactly would be the best time next year for me to come back. "I was hoping you'd say that," he says.

FRESH MONGOLIAN
PRAIRIE DOG BAIT

I came to Mongolia to fly-fish for taimen,
the legendary salmonlike fish that lives in
its big rivers. When fly-fishing didn't work, I
tried spinning with lures. When spinning
with lures got no bites, I tried half a dead
lenok (another kind of fish). When the lenok
was a bust, I went to the can't-miss bait: a
prairie dog. And now, in the last hours of
the last day, the dead prairie dog at the end
of my line was mocking me.

After five hours of continuous casts into
the Delger River without so much as a
nibble, the dog was both absurdly stiff and
unbearably heavy, the twin effects of rigor
mortis and being waterlogged. And even
though it had been dead for almost 24
hours, it somehow stuck its stiff, black
tongue out at me.

Sure, I'm dead, it seemed to say, *but you
are one sorry-ass fisherman. You couldn't
catch a taimen if you were both in the*

same bathtub.

"Shut up," I replied. "I may catch one yet." I took another step downriver and cast once more into the water and started another retrieve. I was so far gone by this point that it didn't even strike me as strange that I was conversing with my bait. Because the dog had a point. I had traveled halfway around the world on the trip of a lifetime, fished my brains out for six days, and been skunked.

The Journey from Moron

Looking back, there were signs — like the name of the Mongolian town from which I embarked on a six-day hunt for big taimen: Moron. But I was too pumped to be suspicious. After reading about taimen for years, I was finally going after one of the least known gamefish on earth. And after 48 hours on airplanes, I had finally made it to Mongolia, one of the most isolated and unspoiled countries on the planet.

The fish that had prompted me to take leave of my senses is an evil-tempered, prehistoric critter that lives only in certain big, cold, fast rivers in Mongolia and Siberia, most of which flow into the Arctic Ocean. *Hucho hucho taimen* is a spotted fish that grows to great size (fish measuring more than 4 feet and 50 pounds are not uncommon).

Because taimen (pronounced TIE-men) live in such remote areas, they are little studied, and sport fishing for them is a recent development. The current all-tackle record, a 92-1/2-pounder caught in Siberia in 1993, is likely nowhere near the maximum size. There is, for instance, a report of a 231-pound commercially caught fish back in 1943. It is an ancient species, the ancestor of modern salmon and trout, equipped with an oversize mouth lined with rows of small, sharp teeth. And it is belligerence personified, cannibalizing its smaller brethren and happily murdering pike, salmon, grayling, small birds . . . and prairie dogs.

I'd read online that Mongolian nomads hook a dog, float it downstream on a shingle of wood, and then give the string a quick jerk. In a typical take, the taimen leaps clear of the water *before* attacking its prey, stuns it with a blow from its powerful tail, and then comes back around to finish the job.

The idea of catching a sociopathic aquatic vertebrate like that on a gentlemanly 9-weight fly rod appealed to me. It would be like putting on a top hat and tails and going 10 rounds with The Rock in a phone booth.

I booked a trip with guide Andrew Parkinson through WadersOn.com, a worldwide fishing resource based in the United States. And now I was bouncing over the Mongolian steppe in a van with him and three other anglers: Greg and Bruce (two Aussies on a six-week fishing trip to Mongolia, Alaska, and the Kamchatka Peninsula), and Steven, a Canadian working in Beijing. Even in my jet lag–diminished state, I was struck by the landscape. But it wasn't so much what was there as what was not.

There were no signs, no fences, no concrete — and, just to keep things simple, no road. Only endless rolling grasslands over which our driver raced. Mongolia, sandwiched strategically between Russia and China, is a huge place, three times the size of France with a population of just 2.75 million, of whom 43 percent are nomadic. Herds of sheep, goats, shaggy yaks, and tough little horses dotted the land.

We passed ancient piles of stones, the altars of invaders who had come and gone as long as 4,000 years ago. Prairie dogs and big marmots streaked for the safety of their dens as they caught sight of the van. Overhead flew ravens and rare white-naped cranes, which number just 5,000 worldwide.

"Just hope Ganchuluun doesn't see a wolf," Parkinson said of our driver. "If a Mongolian in a car or on a horse sees a wolf, he goes a bit mad. And he won't stop until the car is broken, the horse can't run anymore, or the wolf is dead. Mongolians absolutely hate wolves."

We stopped to view deer stones, upright grave markers from the Bronze Age. They all faced south and were covered with stylized images of elk-like deer antlers. On one Parkinson pointed out what he thought was a fishhook. Every few miles we came across gers, the traditional round, felt houses that nomadic herders have been picking up and moving every few months for centuries, forever in search of new grass.

A Log with Fins

We finally got to camp, a series of gers along the banks of the Delger River, late that afternoon. Over dinner, Parkinson told us about the biggest taimen he'd caught. He and a friend had been prospecting a new river when they spotted a log in the shallow water at the head of an island. Logs being scarce in Mongolia, they inspected this one more closely and determined that it had fins. The friend tried to reach it with his fly rod and failed. Parkinson had a spinning rod and cast a mouse lure in front of the fish.

It made the classic taimen attack, leaping clear and clubbing the fish with its tail. Unfortunately, it snapped the 20-pound-test line in the process. Parkinson next tied on a Rapala, and this time the line held. He fought the fish for over an hour as it leapt and raced seven times up and down a side channel of the river. His shoulder and arm went numb during the fight, and his friend massaged them whenever the fish went down to sulk.

At last they fought the fish into shallow water. Because it was too big for their net, they beached it. Parkinson's friend was an experienced angler, but he'd never tangled with a taimen, and Parkinson had to talk him into approaching. They measured it at 53 inches. It broke their handheld scales, which maxed out at 50 pounds. That was when Parkinson decided to chuck his job as a farming consultant back in England and move to Mongolia.

Let the Games Begin

The next day we started fishing. Taimen like big pools and long riffles, Parkinson told us, but since they could be picky, it was necessary to methodically cover every foot of

171

water. We'd be fishing big gurglers, foam-and-bucktail flies that made an appropriately desperate-sounding *plonk* when popped.

All of us piled into the back of an old Zil 31, a six-wheeled army truck that Parkinson said had "fallen out of the back of a Russian army depot" about the time the Soviets pulled out of Mongolia around 1990. We dropped the two Aussies and Edward, a friend of Parkinson's who had come over from England to guide on the trip, downstream. Steven and I got off with Parkinson a couple of miles upstream. During the next eight hours, we experienced a sampling of Mongolian summer: 50-degree swings in temperature accompanied by sun, rain, snow, hail, and winds that rotated through all four points of the compass.

The river was 100 to 150 yards across, but the current in most places was so strong that I found it impossible to wade past my knees. Even though the wind made for tough casting, I managed to work a long pool 30 feet out. The drill was to cast across, strip methodically, let the fly sit for a moment as it dangled at the end of its drift, move a step downstream, and repeat. Steven and I did that for three hours without so much as a rise. Then it was time for lunch.

When the truck rumbled up, Greg and Bruce were already in back, smiling. Each had landed and released a taimen. The bigger, Greg's, had gone 30 inches. "Just amazing, mate," he told me. "Hit it not 4 feet from me at the end of the retrieve and scared me to death. Vicious fish. Took me 15 minutes to land it, and 30 inches is a small one." He reported the teeth to be sharp and numerous and was glad he'd had Parkinson's biteproof fish-handling glove to remove the fly.

Hold the Dog

At lunch in the ger where we took our meals; Parkinson and some of the English-speaking locals he hires gave us a lesson in ger etiquette. Upon entering through the ridiculously low door, you move to your left, clockwise, so as not to impede the universal flow of energy.

You never step on the threshold, touch other people's hats, or use a knife to cut in the direction of any other person. If you spill any beverage, it is customary to immediately shake the hand of the person nearest you. It is considered rude to pass directly in front of an older person, point your feet at the stove, or put water or garbage on a fire, which the Mongolians consider to be sacred.

When approaching a traditional nomad's ger, the correct greeting is *"Nokhoi khor,"* which literally means "hold the dog." A dog in this country is expected to earn its keep, which involves biting the legs off any unknown human. Nyamaa, a beautiful woman who helped around camp and spoke some English, further informed us that women, especially those who are pregnant, do not eat fish. Fish are the only animal that makes no noise, and the fear is that a woman who eats them may give birth to a deaf child.

Witchcraft?

That afternoon, Greg and Bruce both caught and released small (25-inch) taimen. "I don't understand it," Greg said happily over a cold can of Chingis beer. "I'm the worst caster in the lot. I think it's my lucky Filson hat." I smiled. I wanted that hat — I wanted anything that might help me nail a taimen.

The morning of the second day I spent fishing some beautiful water, a bend in a small gorge with very fishy-looking pools. Nyamaa was walking some distance behind to keep an eye on me. The Delger, like most rivers in Mongolia, has few particularly dangerous rapids, but on the other hand it's big water, powerful in places, and cold. If you filled your waders, you could get into trouble a lot faster than you could get out.

I had worked a long section and then walked back up to fish it again. Seated on a rock a little above me, Nyamaa watched in silence. As I passed her, I turned from the river for a moment and teasingly asked, "So what did you do with all the fish?" as if she'd somehow spirited them away. At that instant, as my fly lay motionless at the end of its drift, a taimen hit the lure like a baseball bat and disappeared. Frantic, I cast repeatedly, trying to draw another strike. No dice. I looked at Nyamaa, who was smiling enigmatically. Her poise at that moment was unnerving, almost as though she had known the fish would pick that moment to strike.

My intention all along had been to take the high road, fly-fishing only. By the third day, however, I had begun to slide. I accepted Parkinson's offer of a spinning rod and a large, articulated black-and-silver Rapala rigged with two single barbless hooks. This way I could cover more water and fully expected another baseball-bat strike at any moment. Wading out as deep as I dared toward a bend where a glacier came into

175

the river on the far side, I let fly. As the lure wobbled seductively in a foamy pool, another taimen came up and exploded. It did everything but actually bite the lure.

Again, my efforts to raise a second strike failed. Taimen were aggressive but wary. Parkinson was as disappointed as I was, the sign of a good guide. "My aim is to show every angler a meter-long fish," he said. "Usually, I can. We may have to resort to extreme measures." He gave me a version of his mouse lure, which, when wet, weighed several ounces. I actually threw it over the river and landed it on the glacier, from which I teased it into the water. Still no luck.

At lunch we found out that Greg had hit the jackpot, landing a taimen measuring just over 40 inches and so broad across the back that he couldn't grab it. "I've never seen a freshwater fish like it," he said. While trying to free his lure, he had reached into the fish's mouth with the protective glove. "It nearly crushed me hand," he said, "and bit through the bloody glove like it was paper. Lucky I only got this." He showed a small puncture wound on his finger. I wanted a wound like that, too.

Luck with Lenok

At lunch that day as we sat by the river eating sandwiches, Nyamaa urged me to have a beer. "It will make fish come. I am sure of it." I had the beer. When I woke up, I was lying in the grass and everybody had headed off fishing. Nyamaa was watching me. "You were really asleep. We tried shaking you but you would not awaken. So we take your picture. Did you dream of a fish?" I couldn't remember. She still had that unnerving smile. I got my rod and started casting.

In my obsessive hunt for taimen, I'd been passing up all sorts of other opportunities, from fishing for lenok and grayling to visiting a local village and the gers of nearby nomads. One afternoon, we went way upriver and crossed in a spot so deep that the water came up over the floorboards in the back of the truck and it appeared that we might be stationing a casting platform there permanently. As I walked back to the rendezvous point, I discovered Bruce casting in a pool with a little 5-weight. He offered to let me have a try, and within 15 minutes I'd landed two lenok and two grayling, good additions to the night's dinner. It was also the first tug on my line I'd felt since leaving home. I liked it. Lenok are quite good sport on a light rod, but I was a prisoner to my taimen-mania.

Parkinson, sensing my fixation and my despair, cut the smaller lenok in half and rigged the tail end on his spinning rod with a treble hook. I'd slipped from fly-fishing to spinning with lures to heaving a bloody hunk of fish across the river. It wasn't the first time I'd thrown my dignity out of the boat to lighten the load, and it wouldn't be the last.

You Shoulda Been Here Next Week

On the evening before my last day of fishing, I saw two of the camp boys on horseback trotting swiftly back to camp carrying something hanging from a string. As they got closer, I saw that it was a freshly snared prairie dog. My heart soared. I was so happy I nearly dropped my beer. Prairie dogs are cute little things, and were it not for the fact that they are known to carry bubonic plague and dig horse-crippling holes in the ground, I might have regretted this one's demise.

Parkinson and the boys spent about an hour working on the dog, fortifying its spine and rigging the treble hook until the lure swam with a lifelike motion. They put a good dollop of Gink on the tail to make it float realistically. This, I was sure, was going to be one of those trips that is saved at the last minute with the catching of a tremendous fish. Mine would be a tale told around the campfire for years to come.

Only it didn't turn out that way. I cast that damn prairie dog until we both looked about equally beat up. I never got a bite. As the evening grew gray and the wind came up, Parkinson came and put a hand on my shoulder. "We know there are fish here. And you fished harder than just about anybody I've ever had on a trip." I turned and tried to smile.

The next day, we loaded up and left. The last image I saw of camp was Nyamaa and her benign, knowing smile. We said goodbye at the Moron airport as another group of anglers got off the plane we were about to board.

I got an e-mail from Parkinson the next week. Fishing had turned fantastic right after we left. His four clients landed 18 taimen in five days. Each had one that measured at least a meter. I'm trying to be philosophical about it. I find beer helps.

THE TOUGHEST SON OF A GUN IN THE ELK WOODS

When I first meet Orvall "Junior" Bedell at the tiny airport in Hayden, Colorado, I'm thinking there's been some terrible mix-up. An eastern whitetail hunter, I've just plunked down the money saved by staying out of taverns for 18 months straight to pursue my dream of bagging a bull elk with a bow. And now I'm shaking the square, calloused hand of an old cowboy straight out of Central Casting: spurs, black hat, and a silver belt buckle the size of a cheeseburger that reads, DINOSAUR ROUNDUP RODEO — TEAM PENNING CHAMPION 1994. I don't know what I was expecting. I only know that this is *not* it. "Look," I want to tell him. "Don't take this the wrong way. I like Yosemite Sam as much as the next guy. But what I was really after is a *damn elk guide.*" But I don't because (1) my curiosity is already getting the better of me and (2) the money's gone anyway.

The guy is 60 if he's a day, with a tan that stops where the permanent shade of his hat begins, three toothpicks in the hatband where most guys stick a feather, and mud spatters on his shirt. Plus he's smiling too much. This is not good. Where I come from, smiley people are generally on medication. Stumped for something to say as I stumble toward his truck under the weight of every piece of gear I own, I ask if he still rodeos. "Yep," he answers. "Won a little over seven grand last year." In fact, he's in the middle of a little team cattle penning right now — and he's taking me there.

Junior, a.k.a. the Dinosaur

As soon as we get to the local ring, I can't help noticing that everybody here defers to the dinosaur. A pretty woman atop an expensive-looking piece of horseflesh bats her eyes at him and asks if he can come shoe the beast sometime later in the week. One of the judges takes Junior's arm to speak about something he doesn't want overheard. Even the guy turning the mud to dry before the event swings the tractor by to ask if Junior thinks the harrow is set too deep. I take a seat by the judge he was talking to and mention that Junior seems to be quite the man. "Oh, they don't make 'em like

Junior no more," he says. "You just watch."

He explains that in team penning, groups of three riders race the clock to cut three specific head of cattle out of a herd of 30, then drive them into a small enclosure at the opposite end of the ring. The team members at this club event are chosen at random from a hat. A pattern quickly emerges: The teams that Junior is on tend to win; the teams he is not on don't.

Velcroed to the saddle, he rides at a gallop into the herd and scatters cattle like billiard balls. Then the three he wants trot out obediently and head for the enclosure as if that's where they wanted to be in the first place. His two teammates make a lot of noise and flap their hats at the animals, but it's clear who's getting the job done. At the barbecue afterward, Junior picks up four checks totaling $310 and two belt buckles. It's the last rodeo of the season and everyone teases him about beating up on them all summer. Junior just smiles.

Trophy Haven

"You'll sleep at my place," he tells me back in the truck. Steamboat Lake Outfitters, of which Junior is a partner, has 14,000 acres leased around Routt County, and apparently there's no need to pack into the back-country. "No sense huntin' where they ain't. Elk've mostly moved down out of the national forest. Too much pressure." Junior's house is not really a house. It's a combination antler-storage and used-outdoor-gear facility, with countless rodeo ribbons, three calendars, and a mountain lion skin decorating the walls. His bow is there, an old PSE Polaris Express with round wheels. ("Hell," he says. "Thing's practically new. I don't think I've had it 10 years.")

He shoots fingers without sights. His anchor point is just below his right eye. "I like to look down the shaft to see where it's going." On the wall are Pope and Young certificates for two whitetails and a Rocky Mountain goat. He has too many elk antlers to keep them in the house. When the truck lights raked his garage on the way in I saw heaps of them in the corners and crawl space. He got his guide's license in 1958, when I was 3. I'm beginning to think I've fallen into the right hands after all. "Wake you at 5," Junior says.

At 6 the next morning we are glassing a herd of 160 elk along a riverbottom, already threading their way up through the steep draws on the far side to bed in the hills for the day. Though they're nearly a mile off, their calls and whistles carry clearly. We count only five bulls in the herd. None appear to be monsters, but even through the spotting scope on the truck window it's hard to tell for sure at this distance. "We'll have to hustle to get in front of 'em," Junior says. "Let's go."

I've come to Colorado in the best shape of my adult life, thanks to killer gym workouts and avoiding everything I enjoy. Junior, naturally, smokes two packs a day, drinks his first beer before lunch, and fries his elk and mule deer steaks in butter. But I'll give him this: He waits for me to catch up on hills. At least, most of the time he does.

Back at the Ranch

An hour later, crouched down behind some sagebrush, we're watching cow elk and their calves streaming uphill past us not 25 yards away. Even the calves are the size of shooter whitetail bucks. Junior blows on a tiny cow call held together with rubber bands to calm the elk. They aren't alarmed, but neither are they slowing down. We try four different spots and see elk at two of them, but no bulls. At noon, we hang it up and hike back down.

At a fence crossing, Junior says, "Local feller I was guidin' had a 25-yard shot at a monster 6-point right here last year. It's the only fence for miles, and he hit the top strand of wire." He smiles at the memory, pulls on a cigarette. "That guy's face was long as a well rope all season."

Junior's not being colorful for my benefit. This is how you talk when you were raised on a ranch and had neither plumbing nor electricity until you were 6. "Heck," he tells me. "I never got to town but twice a year till I was in high school. Somebody'd look at you funny, you'd go hide behind your momma's skirts."

In the afternoon, we drive up through quaking aspens, alders, and ferns to a high plateau to still-hunt the woods. Along the way, Junior points to a single stake at the edge of a green field. "We had a house right there. My parents got married in September, and I was born in December. Raised five boys on deer meat and taters. Rode my horse to school every day."

I want him to keep talking. I ask how he learned to shoe horses. He says a neighbor taught him on Junior's own horse, given to the boy for helping a farmer hay all summer. "He did the first foot — made me help him with the second. He and I did the third together, and he made me do the last by myself. I wudn't but 9. Didn't have any money, but I did have sense enough to ask what I owed him. He said, 'Nothin', but don't ask me to shoe your horse again. Now you know how.' Been doing it ever since." He lights another cigarette. "You wanna hear me flap my gums or you wanna hunt an elk?" he asks. Both, actually.

Breaking the Rules

We park in a meadow at about 10,000 feet and slip into the woods. Junior smells of sweat and cigarettes, and wears the same woodland camo day after day. He learned to hunt in the old days, before the scent and camo industries got hold of the sport. "Heck, if the wind's right, the game won't smell you no matter what," he tells me. "If the wind's wrong, they're gonna scent you no matter how much soap and stink you use." I'm thinking how he breaks all the how-to rules I've memorized as though they were carved in stone. And how that garage full of antlers is all the rebuttal he needs.

We move into the woods, sun at our backs, wind in our faces. He points silently to droppings and the big prints in the soft ground. They're only hours old. Junior doesn't move the way I do, all sneaky and tense. He moves casually, as if he's just another animal filtering through the trees. Several times we see cows and spikes up ahead. He blows softly on his cow call, and the elk relax and move on. "Lotta guys would come in here and bugle 'cause that's what they been told to do," he whispers. "Problem is they blow everything out of the woods. You wanna be giving back the same calls you hear." We press on, the woods getting thicker.

Suddenly, Junior sinks to one knee and motions with the hand behind his back for me to come up. Forty yards ahead, two bull elk are raking alder bushes in earnest. One is hidden by the swaying bushes. The other, a 5-point, three times the size of the biggest quadruped I've ever put a pin on, is visible but screened by the alders, except for a foot-wide window at his left shoulder.

"Forty yards," is all Junior says.

I can shoot 40 yards. I've been doing it all summer. But the elk is moving back and forth in the window. From the Cat Quiver on my back, I nock an arrow with a 100-grain Spitfire mechanical on my Mathews MQ1 and stalk forward and right 10 steps. It's as if I'm in a trance. I draw, let out half my breath, settle the 30-yard pin on his shoulder, and release. The arrow is right on the money. He wheels and crashes off. The other bull retreats 20 yards to even thicker stuff, snorts and bellows at us, then leaves.

We never do see that one.

Junior claps me on the shoulder and says, "Now we wait 15 minutes." After 3 minutes, he says, "Time's up."

The blood trail is faint but steady. We find the elk piled up 150 yards away. The rack is a smallish 5×5. Junior guesses him to be 550 pounds, a 2-year-old. Pope and Young may not beat down my door, but I've got myself an elk. It's all happened too quickly, too easily. My picture was that you're supposed to have 9 or 10 near-successes before you get your elk, and here I've bagged one my first day. "You think we should have waited for a bigger one?" I ask.

"Nope. Something like that happens maybe one in 20 hunts," Junior says. "You get a shot like that, you take it."

We gut him, and Junior washes blood over the exposed meat. "Usually I carry pepper in my fanny pack to keep the flies off, but that blood'll harden and protect the meat," he says. "I think our scent will keep anything but a bear from eating on him until we can get up here tomorrow." He cuts off a hunk of tenderloin and puts it in a Ziploc. On the way out, we come across a place where the ground has erupted in yellow chanterelles. Junior fills another bag. That night we celebrate with a little Jack Daniel's and water, fried tenderloin with garlic, sautéed mushrooms with garlic, and garlic bread. "You get enough garlic in you, the mosquitoes'll leave you alone," he jokes. The food is wonderful. You can cut the meat with your fork.

Family Portraits

After dinner, he shows me an old photo of his father with 10 prime beaver pelts drying on round stretchers and one of his grandfather accompanying a young boy biting his lip self-consciously as he leads an old mare, in his hatband a poppy that the war veterans gave out at the Fourth of July parade in Steamboat in those days. He pulls out an arrowhead his father found in the dry mud on the garden plow one time. It's a bird point, the size of a dime. There are about 70 facets on each side, and the thing nearly sparkles in the low light. He tells me about the new people moving in, the fellow who paid $10.5 million for an 800-acre spread that sold for $2 an acre back in the Depression, and about the neighbors up the road who invited him to a picnic and bonfire in which they were burning down the old wreck of a house out back.

"I told them, hell no, I wouldn't come," he says. "That house was hand-hewn, built

189

with broadaxes. I knew Pat McGill, the old Irishman who lived there. He was one of those old-timers I call draft horse-bred. Guys who were out of bed by sunup and worked till dusk every day of their lives. Old Pat had a horse named Charlie. And even when he was 92 years old, he'd go out with that horse and work in the yard. It'd take him all day to dig four postholes. But he was out there. They don't make guys like that anymore."

Junior pulls himself up short, says we'd better get on to bed if we're going to pack that elk out before noon. He's got a place he wants to take me for mule deer tomorrow around sundown.

We bid each other good night. Lying in my sleeping bag in the dark, I'm thinking how lucky I am to be here, how fast the world is changing, how a hunt with an old dinosaur named Junior is something you can't put a price tag on.

THE PROMISED LAND

The masthead of *Field & Stream* magazine is loaded with the names of guys who can make a fire by rubbing two icicles together, catch a tarpon on a safety pin and some pocket lint, or track a squirrel over a rockslide. When the editors want an alternative perspective, they call me.

"Heavey," one purred into the phone not long ago, "we were wondering where an Eastern hardwoods hunter — let's say a guy with more passion than skill — would go to bowhunt the buck of a lifetime." Easy, I said. He'd head for the Promised Land: Buffalo County, Wisconsin. In the last decade this hunk of deer heaven led the nation with 309 record-book deer, almost twice as many as its nearest competitor. "From the numbers it looks like most any bozo would have pretty good odds at a wall hanger out there." I regretted these words even as they left my mouth.

"Good. Then that's where we're sending you." I could hear a group howl of mirth on the other end. Fine. All my life, I've wanted a shot at a big buck. Now I was going to get it. There was, of course, no guarantee. Just because you make the pilgrimage doesn't mean you'll come home a prophet. But I vowed to hunt as hard as possible. If I failed, I meant to go down swinging.

I asked around and heard good things about Buffalo County Outfitters, where Ted Marum says his object is to get each guest at least one opportunity — meaning an ethical and makeable shot — at a good (130-class or better) buck. Over the years, he says, he's been able to hold up his end of the deal 85 percent of the time on 5-day bowhunts. But it's up to the hunter to convert that opportunity, which is another matter entirely.

"Big deer definitely make guys do stupid things," Marum says. Guys from other parts of the country, suddenly presented with a deer that goes 230 pounds on the hoof, take the shot without judging antlers. So they end up with a 2-year-old buck with antlers in the 115 class. "Nothing wrong with that. But we've got bigger deer here."

"Who Kill Them?"

Following directions to Gilmanton, Wisconsin, I pull up at the bunkhouse on November 7 at dusk to find the place deserted, the hunters still afield. Inside, I flip on the lights and find myself surrounded by a herd of wall mounts that look to have been executed for using illegal steroids and calcium supplements. I am transfixed by these swollen necks and antlers. A sprightly woman pops her head in the door to welcome the new hunter. It's Marum's mother, Joanie. What she does not know is that half of my brain has been shut down by the notion that I might take a buck like the ones before me. "These . . . big deer," I stammer. "Who kill them?" (Did I actually say *Who kill them?*)

"Two of them are mine," she says simply. She points out a bow-killed 8-pointer with a goal-post spread, then a 17-pointer with the root ball of a sycamore tree sprouting from his head. "He was halfway across a river going the other way when I grunted him back in," she says proudly. "Just pick yourself a bunk. Ted'll be back soon." She disappears.

By now I am more than a tad spooked. Buffalo County is one of those places where everything seems normal until you find out that water flows uphill there or the local crows wear little yellow vests and caw out soybean futures prices that are always accurate. Here, it's antlers. The Mondovi *Herald-News* gives no more space to the photo of a bowhunter showing off a 28-point buck wearing a snowplow on its head (a potential new state record, I later find out, that green scores 246) than it does to the kids who've won 4-H awards.

And, thanks to Quality Deer Management, the average rack size is rising. Marum tells me county residents used to willingly shoot 130-class bucks. Now they generally let anything under 145 walk. Why run up a taxidermy bill if it isn't something special?

The Meltdown of a Lifetime

Before dawn, Marum drops me off near a stand by a water hole that the deer have been hitting hard at the edge of a long cornfield. I sit with my back to the field, looking down a steep hardwoods bluff. The way you produce big bucks is by taking a lot of does, and in Buffalo County you have to kill a doe before hunting your buck. At 7:30 a.m., a heated-up young buck comes charging down the field behind me, terribly eager to do something, confused as to exactly what that something is, but increasingly sure that it should involve does. He stops, looks around, and charges off in another direction.

I'm sitting in a Lone Wolf fixed stand just 15 yards off the hole and feeling very exposed. At home, I hunt high and in thick cover. Here, the trees are bare and spindly. Fifteen feet up is about as high as you can get, and there's not much of anything between me and the water. That roomful of big heads is evidence that Marum knows how to hunt his own land, however, so I take the only option open, which is to become one with the tree.

At 8, an electric current runs through me as I hear footsteps, then the crunching of stubble. Being deer, the three does come not from the protection of the steep bluff woods I am straining my eyes to dissect but from across the open cornfield to my back. I turn my head at glacial speed to look. They are nervously sniffing where the buck walked and scanning the field. It dawns on me that their biggest fear may not be hunters but being run ragged by overeager bucks. I look at the ground and try to slow my breathing as they move toward water.

When all three are finally drinking, I draw. But my body betrays me. It knows too well that the path to my dream buck runs through the lungs of one of these deer, and it starts to shake. Soon the tree is shaking, too. The deer freeze and look around. A deer in this frame of mind is in no hurry. It is content to lock up and stay there until they take the Christmas lights down back home. I'm still at full draw but deteriorating rapidly. I don't like to shoot at alert deer, but when I can't hold out any longer, I swivel, aim just behind the nearest broadside shoulder, and release.

I have practiced for this precise moment almost daily for six months in my backyard and can more often than not put my first arrow in the kill zone at 40 yards. This one stabs the dirt a foot wide and left of the doe. All three snort, bolt, and lock up after 20 yards, searching for the source of the loud whisper. Stunned at my miss and unable to nock another arrow without getting made, I freeze, too. Over the next 5 minutes, the does, taut as violin strings, make their way back to the hole. Moving as slowly as humanly possible, I ease another arrow from the quiver and manage to nock it.

Then I proceed to shoot and miss twice more at does less than 20 yards away. It's not a textbook meltdown but something far more spectacular; it's the meltdown of a lifetime, breathtaking in its magnitude and totality. Such a failure would be jumping the fence into the field of farce except for one thing: It happened. To me.

To this day, I don't know whether my arrows went wide or high or came out nock-first. I don't know whether I punched my release or the arrows deflected off my arm. I don't even know if I screwed up all three shots the same way or in different ways. Hours later, when I can tell it is time to go because the light is leaking from the sky like stale air from a bad tire, I am still shell-shocked. As I try to climb down, even the tree seems to be mocking me, tugging at my shoulder to stay at the scene of my humiliation. And then I see that it may be easier to descend if I unbuckle my safety belt.

Humble Pie for Supper

When the 10 of us sit down to chicken, mashed potatoes, and gravy back in camp, we go around the table reporting on the day's events. My account — three shots, three misses, standing does, close range, no obstructions — induces a profound silence around the Formica. Having just met, we do not yet know one another well enough to offer the insults and abuse by which men traditionally bestow comfort upon one another. But Marum sees this situation routinely and knows what to do. He clears his throat and says, "Could you pass the gravy, dead-eye? I mean, if you think you can do it and chew your chicken at the same time."

Everybody cracks up. We are, to a man, fools for deer, and we know that looking foolish — sometimes astoundingly so — is the cost of buying into the game. It turns out that another guy had drawn on a huge buck that would have offered a clear shot if he'd moved one step more. But the buck just melted back into the woods. Each of us is lost in his own world, fork absently swirling his mashed potatoes, seeing that buck, stirring that witches' kettle of deer lust.

Moving Up to the Majors

The next day, I sit at another water hole, this one in a cutover that has had 3 years to heal and now offers superior cover and browse. A 6-pointer wanders in at first light, drinks, catches a whiff of something interesting, and breaks off to follow it. For the next 7 hours, I see zip. This, apparently, is not unusual. Marum had told us that the second week of November is the heart of the rut, and often slower than the week before or after because the bucks are locked up with ready does and don't have to travel.

At dusk, a lone doe wanders in to drink. Twenty yards away she stops and stares right at me, as if she knows exactly what a guy with a bow is doing sitting 15 feet up by a water hole. I am thoroughly busted. I'm not embarrassed; I'm hopping mad. But I won't hop. I won't even blink. I won't even bother to shift my eyes a few feet so she doesn't feel their weight, in the hope that she somehow isn't yet positive I'm trouble.

Then a strange thing happens. The doe ignores me. She shuffles a few feet forward and bends to drink. Trembling, I draw, settle my 20-yard pin, and force myself to hold there. She stumbles off 60 yards and goes down. I've got a doe, made the cut. I'm moving up to the majors.

That night one of the guys, Keith, tells about watching two 170-class bucks fight. A female was the cause, and the heavyweights went at it for 20 minutes all around his stand by a ravine in the woods. At one point, they stumbled, fell, and slid 30 yards down the incline, then got up and went right back at it. He never had a shot.

"You saw this today?" somebody asks. Keith hesitates. Actually, he'd seen it the first day. But he hadn't wanted to tell anybody about it for fear he'd lose the stand. We all roll our eyes. Marum has 150 stands on 4,000 acres and just 10 guys hunting. There's tons of space. Besides, no one would think of laying claim to another's spot. But big deer make guys do funny things.

Having taken my doe, I naturally find myself besieged with them on the third day. They file past my stand on a bench on a steep bluff: all big, sleek, healthy ladies. They are hyperalert, and every time they see the one small buck working the woods above me, they freeze, then take off running.

Twelve hours a day in a stand, combined with the knowledge that the buck of your life could arrive, show himself, and depart — all within 5 seconds — wears at a man. Back at the bunkhouse, Pete, who runs a maid service in Ohio, gets disgusted with me when I keep the light on too long looking for the earplugs that are as necessary at night in a deer camp as broadheads are afield during the day. "Damn it, Heavey, will you let me get some sleep?" he bawls. "It's 8:15, for crying out loud!"

Nightmares

On my next to last day, I hike in the dark through a cornfield and up a steep tractor path to a wooded saddle between two hills, then follow the right ridge 200 yards before descending 50 yards to a stand on the back side of the hill. Something about the setup feels right: thick woods near food, trails everywhere, rolling topography. Smells like deer to me. By 7:15 a.m., two bucks have passed in the thick underbrush above me, one of which I would have gladly whacked. I never got a tine count, but he was carrying more antler than any deer I've ever taken a poke at. He knew where he wanted to go, however, and no grunt, bleat, or rattle could entice him my way.

At noon, I make an executive decision. I'm too tired to stay alert. If I take the macho route and stay on stand, I'll be too fuzzy to react if a cruising buck presents a quick shot. On the other hand, if I come down for a half-hour nap, I risk missing a wandering noonday buck, but at least I'll be tolerably sharp for the 6 hours remaining. I descend, find a nice little bed of leaves, and conk out.

Minutes after I regain the stand, the biggest live rack of my life appears, walking the saddle above me. It is Godzilla, abroad in plain day, casually trolling for does. I never see his body or get a clear enough view to count tines. But he is a once-in-a-lifetime animal. Like so many monsters at midday in November, he is moving from point A to point B, and nothing I do changes his mind about it.

Later, after dinner, I go straight to bed. In the middle of the night, I'm awakened by an arm shaking my shoulder. "I don't know who you're fighting with," says the arm, "but it's getting kinda loud." I am sweating, though the room is cool. I lie awake for an hour. I'm not the only one talking in my sleep. I hear a voice suddenly blurt, "Did I miss him? Did I miss him?"

Bottom of the Ninth, Heavey at Bat

For the final day, I move to yet another water hole tucked in some hardwoods below the same saddle. Though water has not yet proved to be the buck magnet I'd hoped for, it still seems like the best move. There are lots of willing does, the deer are already lugging around their winter fat, and autumn has been dry and warm. All that genetic imperative stuff makes a guy thirsty. But I'm feeling more resigned than hopeful as I strap into an oak tree with the wind wafting across the water and into my face. I've never yet pulled a hunt out on the mythical last day.

Around 8:30 I hear the slow, deliberate crunch of leaves that no squirrel can make.

A gray-coated deer emerges from the tangles on the far side of the hole and makes its way slowly in my direction. There are antlers on its head. The antlers have 10 points. The buck is moving slowly but calmly, stopping now and then to look around. It comes over the little berm that is the far edge of the water, 35 yards away. I force myself not to rise or stir.

Satisfied with the scene, the buck now comes straight down to drink. The pond is covered by a thin layer of ice, which he breaks with a few solid taps of his left front hoof. He bends to drink. I rise but do not draw. He is head-on, offering no shot. The rack is typical, not especially tall, but heavy. I guess him to be a 3-year-old. He is not a monster by local standards but he is far and away the biggest buck I've ever seen that I might have a shot at.

He finishes drinking and stands 30 yards off. I draw, sure that he can hear the sound of the arrow as it touches each fiber of my Whisker Biscuit rest. He looks around, deciding which way to go, and in the process turns broadside. I hold the middle pin on his lungs for a long time and, almost reluctantly, let it go.

The buck bounds away over a tiny rise. My arrow lies precisely where he stood, still pointing in the direction I sent it. I grunt and rattle to lure him back. Nothing. After half an hour, I descend. After all that has taken place, I'm almost afraid to look at my arrow. I pick it up and note the expanded blades on the Snyper head, which are red and wet. The shaft appears to have had precisely enough energy to pass through him and not an iota more. There is blood on the vanes. And a spot of it 5 yards away on the frozen mud at the edge of the berm.

Eighty yards away, a 10-pointer with twice as much deciduous bone as any deer I've ever killed lies piled up in some honeysuckle vines.

I crouch down and spend several minutes reassuringly patting this creature's flank. "Thank you," I whisper. And, "I'm sorry." There is the eternal hunter's feeling, the interlocking elation and regret. But this time it's leavened by more than a little humility. I have hunted this deer and found that what I have brought to ground is not only him but a new sense of my own self. I am a guy who is just aware enough to know he hardly understands a thing about deer, who loves the hunt in a way he can't explain, and who — when he succeeds — is never quite sure if it was because of his efforts or despite them. So be it.

Two hours later, Marum is admiring my buck. "That rack's got a lot of character," he says. "It's a fighting rack. Kind of compact and gnarly. Buck could do a lot of damage with that rack." He takes off his glove to shake my hand. Mine still has blood on it. I ask what he thinks it will score. "Oh," he says, "I think he's probably a book deer. If not, he's right on the edge."

I try to keep my smile from taking over my whole face. It's tough. My newfound humility flies out the door and I stand there, feeling unstoppable and confident, a deer-hunting machine if there ever was one.

ICE CRAZY

Until very recently, my entire knowledge of ice fishing came from a story my father told when I was a kid. Driving along the shore of a lake in upstate New York one winter night, he saw the glow of lights from a fish house out on the ice. Never the shy type, he walked out, knocked on the shanty door, and proceeded to spend a very enjoyable few hours drinking beer with the two guys inside.

That tale goes through my mind as I stand in a Wal-Mart in central Minnesota on a cold (what else?) late-January day, trying to find clothes suitable for attending the largest ice-fishing festival in the country, and quite possibly on earth: the 15th Annual Brainerd Jaycees $150,000 Ice Fishing Extravaganza (brainerd.com/ice). The festival draws thousands of anglers from all over the Midwest, who come to compete in a 3-hour contest for more than $150,000 in prizes. Unlike my father's encounter, no shelters are allowed, though I'm pretty sure that if beer were forbidden, there wouldn't be much of a turnout.

Before coming here I had scrounged some gear from Northern Outfitters, a favored brand among Arctic research scientists. The only problem is that all of it except the boots is still sitting 140 miles to the south in the Minneapolis airport, so I'm forced to get replacements here. Unfortunately, thousands of ice fishermen had the same idea a few hours before I did. The place looks as if the "What's-in-your-wallet?" Vikings have already ransacked it. There is as much stuff on the floor as on the racks, and most of the sales staff has fled. Half an hour later I emerge with the following:

- One pair of leather chopper mitts that would have fit Andre the Giant.
- One woman's size XXL insulated polyester shirt, apricot (which the saleslady points out is a really gross color on someone with my skin tone).
- One pair of expedition-weight polypro long underwear bottoms that are so long I could just tie the foot openings shut and forgo socks.
- $44 worth of hand warmers, which I

will affix to various parts of my body with:

- One roll of duct tape.

A Seething Mass of Badly Dressed People

At Gull Lake, the contest site, all worries about being unfashionably dressed vanish. There are people wearing whole bobcat skins on their heads, matching skunk hats and skunk-trimmed boots, fur mittens the size of tennis rackets. I quickly identify the pelts of beaver, raccoon, rabbit, muskrat, nutria, and possum. If it will stick its leg into a trap, you can wear it as a hat to an ice-fishing contest, and most guys leave the tail on to facilitate animal identification. There is a lot of waterfowl camo, blaze orange deer gear, and Carhartt coveralls. The true studs here are strutting around in full snowmobile drag: lime green jacket-and-pants outfits with yellow trapezoid shapes where their muscles would be and armor plates in the shoulders. All they need are ray guns to complete the look.

On the other hand, I'm not going to make any best-dressed lists, either. The three hand warmers I taped over my kidneys have already slid down to a crevice in my body which would be accessible only if I took off most of my clothes, and nobody needs to see a grown man in an apricot shirt. The boots, however, are working perfectly. My feet are so warm that they push a little puff of condensation through the outer boot with each step, which instantly turns white in the frigid air, as if my feet are little choo-choo trains.

Finger-numbing cold and nonstop inaction are not the only things that draw people to this festival. The $150,000 figure in the title refers to the worth of the prizes distributed by the Brainerd Jaycees. Apparently, rewarding skill alone makes no more sense in ice fishing than it does in finger painting, because the Jaycees spread the prizes around randomly and liberally. The angler who catches the biggest fish (which will be a 3.71-pound walleye caught by Sara Kitzman of St. Cloud) takes home a Ford F-150 truck. The 100th-place winner (Jason Himmelwright of Apple Valley, Minnesota, for a 1D 2-pound walleye) will pocket $10,000. And the lucky anglers in 20th, 40th, 50th, 101st, 125th, or 150th place each receive a new Polaris ATV. In other words, a rock bass or a perch that would get lost on a dinner roll could be the catch of your life.

The contest is held on a 250-acre section of Gull Lake. To prepare the area, the organizers drill 24,000 fishing holes, each 8 inches in diameter. It's a process that takes 3 days and massive amounts of Bengay. Thousands of people are out here, some of whom would be pretty hefty naked, let alone wearing five layers of clothing and mammoth Sorel Ice King pac boots, pulling sleds loaded with cases of beer, coolers, portable heaters, radios, lawn chairs, and — in some cases — actual fishing gear. These extra million tons or so cause the ice to sag, which sends lake water gurgling happily up through the holes. In effect, you are walking around in a large, gray Slushie, which within minutes freezes into a topo map of Hell, all knife-sharp ridges and slick hollows. The organizers are overlooking some great possibilities here. A combination three-legged race and EMT-wound-treatment derby would be a surefire way to maintain crowd interest during slow periods.

Proceeds from ticket sales benefit the Confidence Learning Center, a nonprofit organization that helps people with developmental disabilities. Many of us out on the ice appear to be prime candidates for the center. The organizers evidently think so, too, because there are emergency divers from the local rescue squad here, standing around in inch-thick neoprene. I'm sure it's a prudent idea, insurance-wise. But the only people likely to need their services today are those skinny enough to disappear down an 8-inch hole or fat enough to break through 20 inches of ice.

You have to walk a gauntlet of vendors demonstrating the latest gear to get to the fishing area. For a mere seven grand, you can buy the new Wilcraft amphibious vehicle, which is a little fishing shack on wheels. You drive it to your desired spot, pop the top up, and lower the platform hydraulically to the ice with the push of a button. Drill up to three holes through the guides in the floor and you and a buddy are good to go. Thin ice is a worry of the past because the Wilcraft floats and its tires have a paddle-wheel effect in calm water. When you're done, park it in the bed of your pickup and drive home. Or just stay out on the ice until it thaws in spring, then paddle home.

Television improves the quality of any experience, and ice fishing is no exception. The Aqua-Vu Quad 360 displays four images on one screen, giving you a 360-degree view beneath the ice, day or night. If you're watching your pole, you're going to miss strikes, no matter how good your reflexes. Why? Because many "strikes" are just nibbles, and other times a fish will slurp up your bait so quietly you won't even know it. Instead, watch the Quad monitor and see exactly how and when the fish takes your bait, vastly increasing hookups. Since you can also see the baits and fish around other anglers' holes, you may advise them to fish deeper or shallower if they are in danger of succeeding on their own. Used this way, the Quad 360 can pay for itself in increased tournament winnings.

Over by the StrikeMaster ice augers, a big guy with a snarling machine has a crowd around him. It's Sean Spraungel, world-record holder in power-auger ice drilling. In 2004, Spraungel drilled three holes through a little more than 2 feet of ice in an astounding 8.6 seconds. That was using a machine that ran on nitrous oxide, a somewhat unstable fuel that has a tendency to transform a working engine into flying shrapnel. For that reason, Spraungel is using regular gas in an auger with a modified 110cc chain-saw engine today. But he's still astoundingly fast, popping out holes as if he were drilling through Styrofoam. He is a seventh-generation stonemason, 6 feet 7 inches tall and 310 pounds. That size comes in handy during competition, when you have to start with one hand behind your back. He says there are really only two tricky aspects to competitive drilling. One is that the auger is so souped up it pulls the operator down after it bores through the ice. The other is that it's easy to cut off a foot. He shows me a gouge in the sole of his boot, a close call he suffered in practice. A competition auger is a powerful beast and will chew through whatever it gets close to. I don't know what his summer job is, but the guy would be any groundhog's worst nightmare.

Cheers on the Ice

Past the vendors, I need my cell phone to locate Walleye Dan, a local guide who has invited me to fish with his family and friends. He offers me a folding chair, and I skim the ice out of my hole and hook a fathead through the tail. When the noon starter gun sounds, I open the bail and let it fall 42 feet, then crank the reel up a turn.

Within 30 seconds, a strange transformation steals over the crowd. The raucous party atmosphere is gone, replaced by the collective concentration of thousands of anglers, whose consciousness has suddenly narrowed to the 8-inch holes at their feet. Walleye Dan, whose real name is Dan Eigen, has told me to bump my bait against the bottom a couple of times to make the mud puff, then raise it up a foot and give it a jiggle every so often. This is pretty much what every other angler out here is doing, in depths from 15 to 70 feet. The fish, beneficiaries of the most monumental and simultaneous air drop of food since last year, must be stunned. For long minutes, the crowd remains quiet. Then a cheer goes up about 100 yards away, and a man with both hands over his head can be seen lumbering slowly in the direction of the weigh-in station.

Walleye Dan has been ice fishing so many years that he thinks nothing of clearing his hole with his bare hand if a skimmer isn't within arm's reach. Then he nonchalantly shakes the hand in the frigid air, the droplets turning to ice even before they reach the ground. His fingernails are cracked and smashed down to the quick from the endless freeze-and-thaw cycles. He hardly seems to notice and asks his wife, Shelley, for another caffeinated soda so that he may further restrict the blood flow to his extremities. He has three children, all of whom are still too intelligent to be out here. Dan meets with more success than most festival participants. In 14 years, he says, he has caught five fish.

We sit on this endless plain of ice, looking like a nomadic herd of anglers who have momentarily stopped and turned our backs to the wind, trying to gather fish before moving on to the next lake. I watch a guy who evidently cannot locate his party. He picks up a snow shovel from his sled, methodically packs up a mound 2 feet high, and climbs it like a watchtower, lord of all he surveys. Not seeing his friends, he climbs down and resumes fishing.

Another man not 10 yards from me has been down on the same knee for half an hour, jigging his bait every 20 seconds. A boy, evidently his son, sits in a folding chair a few feet away and periodically reels up to recharge his glow-bait with a blue penlight, then drops it back to the bottom. The father disregards the commotion around him: somebody jogging by in slow motion with a fish, a woman towing a sled with bratwurst for sale, nearby anglers firing up gas grills to cook burgers and dogs. I call out to him, asking where he's from. Wisconsin, he tells me, barely turning his head. He and his boy drove down last night, about 400 miles. They'll fish, spend the night, and drive back tomorrow.

The hours tick by. Pam, a woman in our extended party, catches a 3-ounce rock bass and heads off to get in the weigh-in line. I check my minnow, which still has a little wriggle left and is untouched by any fish. Soon the gun goes off, signaling the end of the competition. Everyone gathers up their gear, loads their sleds, and begins slogging back to shore.

Almost everyone, that is. After I thank Dan and head off toward my car, I come upon two guys who are still sitting comfortably by their hole, lines in the water, each holding a fresh beverage, steak-scented smoke rising from a mini charcoal grill. I ask if they've caught anything. "Not yet," one says. "But there's two good hours of fishing before sundown."

Caribou Heaven, Caribou Hell

I had envisioned all sorts of hardships on my first caribou hunt above the Arctic Circle: cold, exhaustion, being constantly wet, even the frustration that comes when you haven't seen a 'bou in three days. What I did not come prepared for is being stuck for half a week in a run-down one-room apartment in an Alaskan village with five strange guys watching nonstop reruns of *Everybody Loves Raymond*. This particular hell is due to the outfitter's needing to catch up with a weather-induced backlog of hunters awaiting transport into or out of the bush.

I am on this hunt at the invitation of a buddy, David Draper, who works for Cabela's, and whom I last saw at an ice-fishing festival in Brainerd, Minnesota, where he had taken off most of his clothes in an effort to raise beer money by posing for photographs. (It is a measure of Cabela's strength that it can dominate the outdoor market with somebody like Draper on the payroll.) At the moment, I'm trying to keep from strangling him. For the last hour, every time the show's laugh track has gone off, Draper has joined in with a reflexive, mirthless, and identical giggle of his own. If it keeps up, I may have no alternative. He now resembles nothing so much as a recently dissected frog, something dead that nonetheless continues to kick if poked in the right spot. And what makes it worse is that the four other guys, whom I just met, don't seem to be bothered by it in the least. Which makes me think they are crazy, too.

Crazy in Kotzebue

Truth is, we've all veered off the track. Kotzebue, which lies a few miles north of the Arctic Circle and is the jumping-off point for a good chunk of northwest Alaska, is a dreary little village of peeling houses landscaped with old shipping crates and rusting heavy equipment parts. We arrived at 7:30 a.m. three days ago on the early flight from Anchorage, expecting to be out of here and into camp by noon. But a previous stretch of bad weather (even by Alaskan standards) had backed up the hunters ahead of us going in and coming out of the bush. So we

218

are sitting in the outfitter's rental holding tank, waiting for the word to mount up that never comes. We drink coffee until noon, switch to beer after, and watch one of three channels on satellite TV all day. We fight over the one bed and floor space each night, listen to sled dogs on short ropes 12 feet outside our window bark all night (average bark rate by my watch: 80 times a minute), and eat gummy, insanely overpriced Chinese food in restaurants run by Koreans (don't ask).

For live entertainment, we wander down to the airstrip to hear the latest horror stories from soggy hunters who can barely restrain themselves from kissing the tarmac as they trip out of single-engine planes. There are two guys from Montana whose pilot took their meat, antlers, and most of their gear on the first flight, promised to be back in two hours, and didn't return for six days. They were reduced to splitting a can of soup and a few crackers for dinner to save rations. "It poured almost nonstop for three days," one tells me. "Just buckets of rain. Whenever there was a break, we'd sprint down the beach and back just to try and warm up." A foursome of hunters from Idaho awaiting their plane on a sandbar got cut off by rising waters, retreating until they ran out of high ground and watched some of their gear float away. Without a satellite phone, they might not have made it. An Alaskan National Guard Black Hawk helicopter was dispatched from Fairbanks, as was a C-130 from Anchorage to refuel the chopper in midair. After picking the men up, the helicopter had to take on fuel a second time in the air before finally making it back to Kotzebue. Even the locals sound impressed by that one.

Seeking a respite from the wind and rain at the strip, I stumble into an outfitter's gear shed and find two guys from New Jersey who are three days late and still giddy at having made it back intact. They lost all their cached meat to bears, which then showed up each night between 1 and 3 a.m., snuffling around just outside their tent. "Wall of nylon isn't much security," the shorter one says. "We'd made trip wires of soda cans with stones in them using fishing line, but that didn't bother them. My buddy got immune to the fear after a while. He'd just roll over, stick his arm out the flap, and fire a .44 mag in the air. Fifteen seconds later, he'd be snoring again. Me, I was scared s — less. I couldn't sleep unless it was daytime." They wish me good luck and hustle off to try to get standby seats on the flight back to Anchorage.

Around noon on the third day we suddenly get the word: There's a weather window and it's our turn. There is an ecstatic fumbling for gear, and we hustle down to the airstrip half-dressed. And then, almost before we know it, three planes bearing the six of us are roaring down the runway almost side by side. Bush pilots do not stand on ceremony, nor do they care greatly for instructions from the tower. The name of the game is to move as much cargo as fast as possible because you never know how long the weather will hold.

Half an hour later, we top a ridge and begin angling down toward an uneven gravel bar in the middle of what we are told is the Eli River. "He's not gonna land there," I say to myself. We are clearly descending into a field of igneous rocks the size of bowling balls. "He's not gonna land there." The aircraft is so packed that I'm carrying my rifle between my knees, and I reposition it so that the barrel will only break my collarbone instead of going through my eye when we crash. I am still chanting my little mantra when we come to a bumpy stop.

The planes dump our gear, roar back into the sky, and are gone almost immediately.

Suddenly, the only sound is the wind. We have engaged Northern Trophy Outfitters for transport, food, and camping gear, but nothing else. We are now on our own.

A Caribou Window

We begin ferrying gear through the freezing water and up to a campsite in the stunted trees. Everybody here is from Nebraska but me. Mark Nelsen and Tom Rosdail work with Draper at Cabela's and have come up on their own dime for a busman's holiday. Jeff Baldridge is a veterinary meds salesman who has a farmer's quiet, no-nonsense demeanor and the air of a guy who knows how to put meat on the ground. Steve Freese is a just-retired captain in the Douglas County Sheriff's Department who plans to hunt and fish his brains out for the rest of his life. He is a heavyset man who moves slowly and deliberately and seems incapable of getting upset about anything less than a triple homicide. All these guys are immensely more likable now that we're working together to set up camp. Plus, there are a lot of animals to go around.

The western Arctic caribou herd is the biggest in Alaska, nearly half a million animals. They are barren-ground caribou, generally the biggest antlered of the three types found in North America. In the fall they meander down from their summer grounds in the southeast part of the Brooks Range and winter over north of Nome. While the legal season goes for months, the practical season is short. Antlers are still soft at the beginning of August and don't harden up until September. The bigger bulls in this area wait until the middle of the month to start moving south toward their wintering grounds. By October there is usually too much snow on the ground for a bush plane to land with tundra tires, but not quite enough for skis. What this means is that the effective season for trophy caribou is no more than three weeks, sometimes a month. We're lucky to be here at all.

I find myself in the unusual position of being the most experienced caribou hunter in camp, having once gone after them in Quebec. What I know is that they are tasty but neither particularly bright nor great rewarders of hard work. If you're in an area through which they are migrating, your chances of success are high. But the ancestral travel routes they have to choose from are almost without number, and they make their selection according to criteria known only to themselves. In short, timely local intelligence is everything. When you do get between them and a place they want to go, you're as likely to shoot one close to camp as 3 miles away, though from the way the Cabela's boys are talking, it sounds as if they are trending toward the heroic, planning hikes up into the shale foothills and mountains above the tundra that lie along the river.

Because of the delay getting into the bush, and because I was naive enough to plan another trip on the premise that I could choose the days of my arrival and departure, my five-day hunt has now dwindled to two. The others will stay on, but a plane is to pick me up on Wednesday in time to make the evening flight from Kotzebue back to Anchorage. I am more than a little worried about the brevity of the hunt, but there's not a hell of a lot I can do about it now.

Why It's Called Barren Ground

The next morning, we head out in two groups. Tom, Steve, and I make our way straight up from the dwarf trees into the rolling tundra; the others head north and into the foothills. I thought I had walked tundra on my previous hunt, but the Canadian stuff was asphalt road compared to this. This is boot-sucking, fall-inducing, forward-movement-arresting muck. You start out stepping on the firmer-looking clumps of grass to avoid sinking in the sludge around them. After a few tumbles, however, you realize that the tussocks are a sucker's bet, floating islands you slide off of. So you seek out the lowest ground first, since that's where you'll end up anyway. But even this is a delusion, as the terrain is honeycombed with the hidden trails and burrows of lemmings, voles, and Arctic hares. Every so often you end up thigh-deep in some rodent's condo. It seems entirely possible to disappear quietly and permanently into the ground while the guy in front of you walks nonchalantly away.

After 200 yards, I am winded and struggling to keep up with Tom, who is my age but far more determined. Steve, carrying a muzzleloader, has already fallen 100 yards behind us and is in no great hurry to twist a knee. Tom grimaces. "I think Steve's gonna hold us back a bit," he says when we finally take a break. "Yeah . . . ," I pant. "Steve . . . hold us back." He waits for Steve as I slog another 50 yards to top a rock mound for a look. My Bushnell Elite 10×42s clearly show a herd of caribou on a hill at least 2 miles south. In this kind of walking, and with absolutely no cover for an approach, they might as well be across the Bering Sea.

Steve announces he is happy just to sit on the rock mound and see what develops. Tom and I slog on across the hill, traverse a little creek, and head for a higher perch 500 yards away at the foot of the shale mountains. From there, we can glass, see if they'll come our way, and possibly intercept them. The 20-knot winds slice through us and buffet the spotting scope on its tripod. At 60-power I can just make out the bodies of the older bulls, larger and whiter than the other animals, with shaggy dewlaps. It's tough to get a feel for racks at this distance, and the scale and austerity of the landscape are, frankly, mildly terrifying.

The distant herd continues to feed but does not really move. Several times an hour, Tom and I take short walks below our observation post to keep the blood moving. On one, we suddenly catch sight of five caribou, three females and two juvenile bulls, coming our way from above and left on the mountain. They will soon pass within 200 yards. We hunker down and watch, fearful that spooking them will start a chain re-action. Meat on the hoof, they amble along, grazing the lichens and late blueberries. Their antlers are bigger than those of any deer I've ever shot, but as caribou go they are negligible. After three hours, the herd, including what I can now tell are eminently shootable bulls, is no closer. With the light leaking from the sky, we slog home.

Camp Meat, Part 1

Back at camp, David and Jeff are warming themselves by the fire, both having taken bulls a couple of miles from camp. Their faces tell of satisfaction and exhaustion, initial euphoria followed by five hours of dressing, quartering, and hauling meat and antlers. Steve, the slowpoke, is the only one who has husbanded enough energy to cook. He shaves long strips off one of the fresh tenderloins, seasons them with garlic salt and pepper, and threads the strips onto green poplar sticks. We eat it hot off the fire with our hands, accompanied by the choice of beer or Canadian whiskey.

It sounds picturesque, but our camp wouldn't make it into an outfitter's catalog showing the romance of the wilderness. It's nothing more than three two-man domed tents crammed in among the poplars and spruce, strewn about with waxed cardboard boxes containing our canned goods, perishables hanging in plastic tarps and bags from trees just downwind. But a smoky fire and a damp log to sit on are welcome after a day on the tundra, as is the caribou. It's hunter's meat: flesh that was walking hours earlier. Camp falls quiet while the butt of one of the logs slowly turns into a mosaic of glowing orange tiles that crumble, one by one, into the fire. And one by one, we finish up and crawl off to our bags.

Camp Meat, Part 2

In the morning, heading down to the river for water, I take my rifle and remember to walk loudly, recalling the outfitter's advice about bears. "Keep your meat and latrine downwind of camp. Make noise when you go to crap or get wood. Anybody with half an ounce of common sense should be fine." *Well,* I think, *that lets me out.* On top of this, I'm lightly gunned: a Winchester .270 with 130-grain Ballistic Silvertips for "light, thin-skinned game." It's plenty of gun and lead for caribou, and just enough to seriously aggravate *Ursus horribilis.* On the other hand, who am I kidding? A charging grizzly can outrun a quarter horse over the same distance. The best hope for a guy with my combination of nerve and shooting skill is that the bear will be put off by the poopy smell emanating from my trousers.

I'm halfway done filling the big jug before I see it in the black sand by the water's edge. At my feet is a print as big as my size

12s, only twice as wide, and belonging to someone in serious need of a toenail overhaul. It's a griz, and it's popping fresh. I stare at it, wide-eyed, and am instantly transported back 10,000 years. Deep inside my monkey brain, a circuit connects and the ancient warning courses through my bloodstream: *You not top predator here.* We've been told that the bears in this area get hunted hard and generally avoid humans. But if ever I needed a reminder that we are on the unpaved side of the guardrail, this is it. My heart tachs up to about 130 beats per minute. I walk very loudly back to camp and whistle as I go.

A Bull in the Scope

It seems ridiculous (and will turn out to be more ridiculous still) that the second day of the hunt is my last. Tom, Mark, and I head back up to glass in the foothills of the shale north of camp. There are ancestral trails all around and above us: on the ridges, along the river, through saddles. There is even a caribou interstate heading diagonally up the slopes to a very high pass in the mountains some miles distant. It glistens silver in the sun, like a fresh scratch in old lead, traversing a grade where a single misstep would send you tumbling thousands of feet. The only drawback at the moment is that there is not a caribou in sight.

The three of us hunker down out of the wind in the lee of a boulder, slam some energy bars and water, and try to figure the best move. Tom wants to continue north alone to prospect. Mark and I decide to try our luck back south, nearer to camp. In the folds of the foothills there are two streams running from the mountains down to the river. The 'bou use them as travel routes, and any animals spooked by one of our party higher up might be ambushed here as they flee. As we make our way down through a meadow, however, we spot a herd that has moved into the tundra belt above camp in the two hours since we left. Sure enough, they are feeding slowly toward one of the streams. "If we really book," says Mark, "we could sneak up the stream and have a shot if they stay put for a bit." It's a lot of running and only a slim chance at gunning, but that's what we're here for. We set out at maximum slog, pushing hard just inside the cover of the trees at the meadow's edge, sneaking out now and then for an update.

We duckwalk low up the streambed, only 500 yards from the herd, in which we now can see several shooters. But a shot above us in the mountains seems to unnerve them, or maybe they've caught a whiff of something. They start to break up. Mark wants to stay put in the hope that they'll regroup.

Mark, I salute you. But you have three more days and my ears are already stuffed with David E. Petzal's delighted howls. "You whiffed on caribou, the highest-percentage of all big-game hunts? I know dead guys who have gone on caribou hunts and scored!"

So I backtrack down the creek to the trees, head south for a few hundred yards, and edge up a little fold in the terrain to another rock mound. My reasoning is simple: A few animals seem headed that way and I can't think of anything else to do. I stalk the area, hoping to see something good when I finally poke my nose over the crest. The wind has risen to 15 or 20 knots, the sky has darkened, and intermittent rain hits my face like needles. I set the .270 before me on its bipod and make like a log, hoping a caribou will venture within range. Half an hour later, the only things that have changed are my body temperature and the amount of daylight remaining. I back down out of the wind for a minute to regain feeling in my feet and hands, wondering whether the sins I'm being punished for are from this incarnation or an earlier one.

And that's when the Tooth Fairy finds me. Directly behind me, less than half a mile downwind, stands a herd of 40 animals or more grazing in the longer grass near the river. I have no idea how long they've been there. I was so sure that anything downwind would take off that I had not bothered to monitor that direction. It makes no sense — but then again it doesn't have to. Because there they are. Better still, although they aren't moving much, when they do it's in my direction. There is a lot of open ground between us, and nothing but a thin belt of knee-high shrubs 50 yards away for cover. If I can somehow get there undetected, I've got a chance.

Dumping my pack, I sling my rifle over my back and start a fast crawl on hands and knees. Every few yards, I fall face-first into the soft, wet moss. My gloves are gone, my boots are full of water, and I have dirt in my teeth, but I am thankful beyond all reckoning to have electrical-taped my rifle muzzle. The wind is still perfectly wrong, but the herd continues drifting in my direction. I put my rangefinder on the lead animal: 273 yards. This is a reasonable shot for an experienced, competent marksman, and I wish I had one along at the moment. I am a mediocre shot on a good day, and this — heavy wind, rain, a body shaking from cold and adrenaline — does not really qualify.

I move again, then once more, until I am out of stalk-sustaining shrubbery. A few of the animals seem to have noticed me and have slowed but are unalarmed. Perhaps I am blessed with body odor that is agreeable to caribou. Or maybe, though they are not God's brightest creatures, they can somehow intuit hunters who can't shoot worth a damn. Meanwhile, the bipod keeps sinking into the muck, giving me a steady bead on the ground 2 feet away. What I need is a rodent hole I can sink into so that the rifle will be higher than my body. But, like cops, rodent holes are never around when you need one. At last, still crawling, I stumble into a wet depression and kick away at it until it accommodates my shoulders. My butt is elevated provocatively, my back is bent like a Cheez Doodle, but none of this matters because there is a bull caribou clomping along in my scope.

I've got more experience driving chariots pulled by matched teams of racing squirrels than I do shooting moving targets at a distance, but it's now or never. I laser him at 170 yards and focus on swinging through as I let out a breath and squeeze. The report scatters the herd. I run the bolt while trying to reacquire him. The bull has stopped and is swaying on his feet with lowered head. Another shot anchors him.

I slog over in a sort of dream state. He is the whole package: more than 300 pounds, thick tawny antlers, the cinnamon coat, white mane, and dewlap common to the older bulls I've glassed. I kneel and stroke his flank and tell him I'm sorry for having taken his life. And then I scan the horizon for hunters and bears. Seeing neither, I prop my rifle close by on its bipod and set to work.

Going Nowhere Slowly

The next morning, as I'm packing up for my flight, a plane from another outfitter flies low over our camp, which I figure is a heads-up that my ride is on the way. I continue to think this right until dark, at which time I unpack and drink beer. This pattern of activity continues for the next two days. I have had the foresight to bring no reading material whatsoever, so I spend most of my time collecting wood, tending the fire, and reading the fine print on the granola bars, Pringles, and soup cans in camp. Occasionally, there is a trip out to haul caribou quarters. Draper wounds a bull one day and, while following the blood trail, notices a blondish grizzly, most likely a large juvenile boar, which has smelled blood and decided to participate in the search. At this point, David decides that the polite and wise thing to do is to let the bear take over. He hustles back to camp with his rifle unslung, walking backward most of the way.

Three days after my scheduled departure, on the day the rest of the party is due to be picked up, we haul everything down to the river and wade back through the water, now half a foot higher, to the gravel bar, leaving only our bags, rifles, and one tent at the campsite. We consider ourselves old Alaska hands now, sourdoughs almost, and know that the plane may fail to show. Which is exactly what happens. Fortunately, we are prepared. We have prudently used up all our firewood and are also out of boiled drinking water. We have wisely moved our cots, without which sleep is nearly impossible, to the pickup spot, along with almost all the food. Remaining at the campsite are two spoons, a big can of beef stew, a roll of toilet paper, and whiskey. We cobble together a fire, roll the can of stew in, and wait until we are reasonably sure that the bottom is burnt and the top is cold. Then we sit by the fire, open it, and pass it from man to man, followed in short order by the whiskey. At a certain point, the liquor laps the stew, then laps it again. The smoke, held down by low barometric pressure, visits each hunter in turn. It's democratic smoke, making sure everybody gets a good whiff. We are too cold and tired to move out of its way. You just sort of try to put your head in your armpit until it moves on to the next guy.

Aside from the exhaustion, soreness, smoke inhalation, and missed flights, we're all feeling pretty good. We are in no particular hurry to return to our cubicles and mortgages. We're lucky enough to be AWOL from our daily lives and adrift in a world with a much stronger claim to reality.

One by one, we crawl into the tent, all of 9 feet square. It just manages to hold six if we lie four across the middle, head to toe, with a man lying crosswise at each end. Roots assault us through our thin sleeping pads. Each of us is getting involuntary acupuncture treatments, mine in the small of my back and left shoulder. Each is also convinced he is sandwiched between the group's two most objectionable hunters in terms of body and breath odor, snoring, and general personality. The darkness fills with groans, complaints, and audible farting as we all struggle for positions that might allow actual sleep. "Cowboy up!" Tom finally mutters. "I've had it worse than this." I have too, I suppose, though it's hard to remember when. Now that I think of it, the nights back in Kotzebue were worse. More comfortable physically, but that was before I knew and liked these idiots, before we had forded rivers and hauled caribou quarters and eaten burnt stew together.

"Gimme another shot of that whiskey," calls Mark. "Why?" someone asks. "Because I'm sleeping next to Draper and he's starting to look good." Steve touches off a silent one that has the guys closest to him burying their faces in their bags for protection. "Funny, I don't smell a thing," he murmurs placidly. The Fall Asleep First Contest, unique among human competitions in that the winner never knows of his victory, is under way. Steve is looking very strong, already snoring, though surprisingly lightly for a big man, as if he's trying to be considerate even in slumber. Jeff keeps skimming just into sleep and out again, a stop-and-start sort of snore. David mumbles that a lit match would blow us all to hell right about now. I find that by turning on my side, wedging a boot under my temple and a spare watch cap under my hip, I can reduce the root pressure to near tolerable levels, as long as I take hourly sips of whiskey. But the noise of snoring and groaning precludes rest for me.

Eventually, I chew up a piece of cardboard packaging that once held chocolate pudding and cram the warm, wet pulp into my auditory canal. At last, I let go and fall slowly into another rodent hole, this one filled with sleep. As I tumble into slumber, I have the half-conscious notion that it's all a question of knowing how to recognize moments of good fortune, that there is always some kind of luck hanging around for those who can see through its strange disguises.

A Hunter's Heart

If you're looking for an unlikely pair, match
the fresh-faced girl with two earrings in her
right ear sitting with the cowpuncher with
the droopy gray mustache, sweat-stained
hat, and dusty jeans. He is leaning more
than halfway over the coffee table in the
windblown desert town of Rock Springs,
Wyoming, here in the lobby of the Best
Western, and holding both her hands in his
upright palms. He holds them like precious
things he might break were he not careful,
and behind a three-day stubble and his
weathered features, he is smiling so hard as
to be on the verge of tears. "I been looking
forward to this more than any hunt I've
booked all year," he tells her. "We're gonna
get you a good deer, honey. I promise you
that. You'll see hundreds of deer. They're
moving down off the mountains now, coming down into their winter range. The big
ones tend to move last. Oh, honey, I'm so

glad you're finally here."

He turns and smiles at the girl's father, sitting next to her on the couch. "You have to hunt with me . . . forever. Every year. You and your dad. On me. Understand?" She blushes, glows, looks at her father, then back at the cowboy. He is serious. She hardly knows him, but he is, here and now, making a commitment that will last as long as either of them lives. The cowboy drops his eyes for a moment, giving her time to take it all in. But she doesn't need time. She neither flusters nor embarrasses nor flees to the safety of a polite protest that it is too great a gift. She smiles. He coughs, then continues in a different tone. "Now, it's okay to spend a little time with this fellow," he says, cocking his head in my direction but keeping his eyes on her. "Just remember," he says, slowly tapping his chest with a forefinger, "I'm your number one." His eyes are watering again. The gray mustache that obscures his mouth stays put while the silk bandanna around his throat rises once and then settles back into its place.

Her eyes dance and change with the light, sometimes hazel, sometimes green. She is beautiful. Her metal crutches lean against the back of the sofa. She has been waiting for this moment forever, nearly 10 months, since last winter at a sporting show in Grand Rapids, when her two brothers wheeled her by the booth of the outfitter who had agreed to work with the Hunt of a Lifetime charity. That was when the man asked her and her father to be his guests for a mule deer hunt. Her name is Alyssa Iacoboni and she is 15 years old. Her head is smooth. Her eyebrows and eyelashes are gone. The chemo took them all (although she insists that a few eyelashes are already growing back). It is as if her head and face in their unashamed nakedness permit her beauty to shine stronger. She is unselfconscious about her appearance: her lack of hair and the stump of leg that stops above where her left knee once was. She smiles and talks freely. Yet she holds within herself a world that is hers alone. Later, photographer Erika Larsen and I will discover that we both thought of Vermeer's famous painting *Girl with a Pearl Earring* upon first seeing Alyssa. In that picture a similarly luminous girl has just turned her gaze to the viewer, as if someone has just entered her room. Vermeer chose to portray his girl without hair, too, though hers by virtue of the blue and gold cloth that covers it completely. It is a trick the artist used to draw your eye to her expression. Both share that startling combination of openness and self-containment, present and vivid, yet reserving unto themselves a mystery.

Vermeer's picture, often dubbed the Mona Lisa of the North for its haunting beauty, was done more than 300 years ago. Alyssa Iacoboni (Yak-a-Boni) is right here. And if she bears a wisdom beyond her years, she is also very much a 15-year-old girl. "I am so psyched to go on this hunt," she says. "My brothers are totally jealous." Just two weeks ago, she killed her first whitetail, a doe on 37 acres the family owns not far from home in Grand Rapids. Her father, Evan, says she is weary from the trip, from delays that caused them to arrive at 4 a.m., instead of 10 p.m.

The next morning, we caravan to the unit where the outfitter, Bruce Feri, who runs Canyon Creek Outfitters, has a special tag for Alyssa's buck. It's high desert country, about 7,500 feet, an endless undulating carpet of sage west of the never-ending spine of the Wind River Mountains. We load up in trucks and head up into the hills to glass for deer. Alyssa is being fitted for a hydraulic leg but is still on crutches at the moment. She hops nimbly into the cab and stows them beside her. I ask about the doe she took. "I'd taken my hunter safety even before I got sick, but didn't have a chance to hunt until this year. First I was nervous when I went out with my brothers. I was afraid I might not like hunting as much as they did. But when I saw that doe, I got so excited I could hear my own heart. It was so intense. And then I made a good shot with the .30/30 and I was even more excited. It was just really cool." She has been practicing with a .22 magnum, and her brothers helped her sight in the new .308 that Savage Arms donated to Hunt of a Lifetime.

There was already a foundation, Make-A-Wish, for young people facing life-threatening illnesses. In 1996, it granted a seriously ill Minnesota boy's wish to hunt Kodiak brown bear in Alaska, a gesture that enraged animal rights groups, prompting them to mount a national campaign against Make-A-Wish. Some members were threatened with bodily harm. When Tina Pattison, a school bus driver and mother of six in Erie County, Pennsylvania, told the group that her son Matthew, an 18-year-old with Hodgkin's disease, wanted more than anything to hunt moose in Canada, she was told the foundation could no longer grant such wishes. It simply wasn't safe. But Pattison was not the type to be intimidated. She and her husband, Chester, got mad.

Then they got on the phone. In time, thanks to the hard work of his parents and the generosity of some outfitters, a lodge, a grocery store, and countless others, Matthew and his dad went on the hunting trip and bagged a 55-inch moose. The anticipation of the hunt kept him going through months of pain, Tina says. "He kept saying, 'I'll be all right because I'm going on that moose hunt.'" Matthew died in April 1999, at the age of 19. And Tina founded Hunt of a Lifetime to honor Matthew's memory and to grant the wishes of other youngsters who love hunting and the outdoors.

As we drive and glass muleys tucked away in the sagebrush, Bruce explains that this is the Sublette herd, the most migratory deer in the West. They travel up to 100 miles from the Salt River, Wyoming, Wind River, Gros Ventre, and Snake River ranges to winter in the desert of the Green River Basin. "They'll stay around here as long as the wind blows the snow off the vegetation. If the snow gets too heavy for that, they'll just keep heading south. Come spring, they'll follow the snow line back up into the mountains." The deer have a tough life, he says. "Sometimes it gets to 40, 50 below up here. That's without windchill. It doesn't stay that cold for long, but they can't stand it for long, either. Come spring, most of these deer are hanging on by their fingernails." The state recently pushed back the date that shed hunters can start walking in this area in the spring for fear of stressing the deer at a critical time. Alyssa doesn't say anything, but she has some experience of her own at the margins, the places where the distance between life and death is as thin as onion skin.

Bruce stops the truck and pulls out a spotting scope. It's a bright, windy day in the low 60s, warmer than usual, warmer than he'd like. There was a dusting of snow a few days ago. He points out four groups of muleys dotting the landscape, numbering nearly 50 in all. "Now let's see if we can find you a good buck." He glasses about six, all with does. It is just before the rut, the females not yet ready but tolerating the bucks, which merely jockey for position rather than fight. Bruce gives his 10-power Swarovski to Alyssa and shows her a bedded 4×4 nearly half a mile away. It takes her a while to see the gray deer hiding in plain sight. "I see him now," she says. Bruce clucks his tongue, thinking it over. "He's not bad, but we can do better." He shoves the truck back in gear.

Until she was sent the terrible blessing of

cancer, Alyssa had been just another normal — if abnormally successful — schoolgirl. She was popular, the girl elected to represent her class at the homecoming dance, an athlete who played basketball and volleyball and ran track. She was the fastest kid in her junior high, just half a second off the school record in the 200 meters. High school coaches were already scouting her. She also did the long jump and shot put. I tell her that she looks too light to be a shot-putter. "Yeah, I know. Everybody thinks it's about upper body strength, but it's more about using your body the right way, momentum and leverage." Her brothers, Daniel and Justin — both jocks, both lifelong hunters, and both set on becoming sheriff's deputies — helped her learn that.

Then one day she came home from basketball camp complaining of pain in her left leg. At first the doctors just thought it was hyperextended and counseled rest. Eventually, they X-rayed it and saw the tumor in her knee, an aggressively cancerous mass in the bones. They scheduled her for an appointment with the oncologist for the next day and gave her a name for the disease: osteosarcoma, bone cancer. Two weeks later she was on her way to Detroit for her first surgery.

Another hour into the hunt, the sun high now, Bruce spots a better buck in the company of about 10 does. A subordinate buck lingers in the brush nearby, causing the big one to assert his dominance and move the ladies. The smaller male invariably shadows them. "Good and bad," Bruce says. "They're moving, but distracted enough that we might get close." He, Alyssa, and I aim for a rock that would give her a decent shot, but soon 12 pairs of eyes have us pinned. Then they take off running. "Don't worry," Bruce tells her as she swings her way back on the crutches. "We'll get you one. You feeling tired or anything?" She shakes her head. "I'm fine."

The diagnosis changed everything. It was as if a portal had opened into a parallel universe, a world invisible to those who live on the surface. All at once Alyssa could no longer measure joys and sorrows by a schoolgirl's standards: cute clothes and the coolest ring tones, popularity and which group you were going with to the football game. When the social worker assigned to her case asked if the idea of dying scared her, Alyssa confronted her parents. Were they keeping something from her? No, honey, they said. We'll never keep anything from you. They told her that her cancer was serious, possibly terminal, but that they would take things one day at a time. She understood that she was in a fight for her life. The possibility of death, someone wrote, tends to focus the mind rather intensely. Alyssa seemed to decide quickly that she still had the three things that mattered most to her: her family, her faith in God, and her belief in herself. That was not to say there weren't times she cried, times she lashed out at her parents, or times when she despaired. But for the most part she showed what many kids show, only more of it: an acceptance of the situation and its possible outcomes that an adult can only envy, and a resolve to fight. "I just realized it wouldn't do any good to be negative," she says. "It doesn't help, doesn't make you stronger. It's like when you're behind in a basketball game. You just focus on what you need to do to get back in it."

Her faith had always been important to her, and it became even more so now. Nearly every day she would recite her favorite verse, 29:11 from the book of Jeremiah: "For I know the plans I have for you," declares the Lord, "plans to prosper you and not to harm you, plans to give you hope and a future." She was in God's hands. Whatever happened, it was what He had chosen for her. She could live with that. If necessary, she could die with it.

We drive some more, stop and eat sandwiches, chew and look at the country. It's sparse and clean and pitiless. Alyssa seems at ease but doesn't say much, doesn't readily reveal herself. I will wonder about this so much that I will call her mom, Linda, after the trip. She will tell me her daughter's composure unnerved her as well. "At each new turn in her illness, she was like, okay, let's fix this and keep going. She is incredibly competitive, I can tell you that. The coaches always had her run anchor for the 400- and 800-meter relays, both for her speed and because she absolutely refuses to lose." During Alyssa's last race, she tells me, the girl handing her the baton dropped it before the pass. "But it was still in the lane, so Alyssa picked it up. And I remember feeling the crowd's reaction, how they didn't think she could catch up. But she did. And she won. She has always been the kind of girl you don't want to say, 'I bet you can't' or 'I dare you' to. She's not insecure, but she has always lived her life like she's got something to prove."

The doctors eventually told her they needed to take the leg. She was offered "limb salvage," in which a combination of cadaver bone, metal rods, and bone grafts enable a patient to keep an arm or leg. But she wouldn't be able to run on such a leg, and there were other risks: increased chance of the cancer recurring and of infection, loosening of the implanted bone, and mechanical failure. On December 7, 2005, she let surgeons amputate her left leg above the knee. She also underwent intensive chemo, six rounds of three treatments each. Chemo, she tells me, is as much torture as it is therapy. The poisons kill the cancer cells, the fastest-growing ones in the body, but they kill everything else as well. The theory behind it is brutally simple: Inflict as much destruction upon the body as possible while still leaving the subject "viable." As soon as the patient has recovered from the last round to the point where she can be expected to survive more, more is administered.

Alyssa became so sick that her mother figures she attended school a total of 10 days during her ninth-grade year. She took drugs to flush the chemicals from her body between courses of chemo, drugs to cope with the excruciating "phantom pain" from the nonexistent leg. The human brain, perhaps perceiving that a limb has been chopped off, reflexively responds, activating the nerve cells in that area to register a traumatic event. Her immunity plummeted to nothing, leaving her defenseless against normally mundane maladies. A nosebleed might last for eight hours and require an emergency trip back to the hospital for a transfusion. Sores in her mouth and nasal passages became infected and required intravenous antibiotics and morphine. She seemed to live at the hospital. Her sense of smell and taste became abnormally acute. The odor of hospital food made her ill. Liz, a 17-year-old friend she had made in the hospital who had a more advanced form of the same cancer, died. "It was hard" is all she'll say. She doesn't dramatize the death, doesn't choke up about it for your benefit, doesn't use it to make some point about her own suffering. "It was hard when Liz died," she says. She reminds me of soldiers I've talked to who have survived extended combat. Such men tend to be low-key to the point of self-effacement. They have transcended any need for the approval — or even the attention — of others. Any questions about their identity, or worth, or place in life have already been settled. They know that each breath is a gift.

Bruce abruptly stops and brings his binocs

up to his eyes. "Shooter buck," he tells me. He backs the truck slowly and angles it to get his window broadside so he can put the spotting scope on the buck. "That's the best one I've seen in a while," he says. Two bucks and two does are feeding about 500 yards away. Studying the lay of the land, however, we see there is no good approach. They are on a little ridge in the sagebrush, higher than everything around them. "Have to throw the dice," he says. Our only option is to drive a little closer before making a right that will take us into a fold in the land from which we could sneak on them. "If we could get to that rock over there," he says, pointing to a boulder, "we might be close enough for a shot." He creeps forward and makes the right, then moves steadily onward. The deer do not take alarm. After a few more minutes, they all bed down: two does about 25 feet away from the bucks, the second of which is much smaller. We get out the .308 and a tripod to steady it on. Bruce asks Alyssa if she can crawl the last 50 yards to the rock or if she'd prefer to be carried. "I can crawl," she says.

"I'm gonna hustle up to that rock, make sure they're not spooked, and try to range 'em," says Bruce. Alyssa hops down from the cab and gets her crutches. I sling the gun across my back so I can crawl when we get close. We set off, Alyssa planting her foot, then swinging forward with her crutches. Each time she moves them, she swings them either around or between the crackly sage tufts to avoid unnecessary noise. I walk doubled over, staying as low as I can. We travel for about 100 yards this way toward Bruce, who is pressed to the rock, his hat on the ground behind him, rising as slow as a snake to peer over with his binocs. He drops back just as slowly, gives us a thumbs-up, and motions that we'll have to cover the rest of the distance prone. Alyssa balances on her foot as she places the crutches quietly on the ground. Then she lowers herself down to her two elbows and one knee and begins to pull herself over the ground.

At last we make it to Bruce and the rock, which is barely big enough to screen us even if we bunch up. Bruce whispers for the shooting tripod, but we have left it behind. I take off my parka and pass it forward. He folds it across the rock. I insert the clip, quietly chamber a round, check that the safety is on, and pass it forward. He helps Alyssa squirm into a shooting position, sitting on her folded knee. All four deer are bedded now, the two does to the right of the bucks. The little buck is bedded left of the bigger one and is easier to see. Bruce wants to make sure she is sighting on the bigger one. The sun is nearly in front of us, and she is having trouble seeing through the scope because of it. At last, she says, "Got him. Oh my gosh." Bruce claps her gently on the back. "We've got 'em where we want 'em, honey. That is a really nice buck. You just try to stay on him." He looks again through his glasses, then ranges the buck. "Two hundred yards," he says. He tells her to relax. We just have to wait now for the buck to get up and offer a good shot.

Minutes pass. Bruce is in an awkward position and needs to drop down and rest every so often. He tells Alyssa to stay on the buck, to wait until he rises and turns broadside, then to shoot just behind the front leg and midway up the body. I sneak a look and watch through the glasses as the big buck lays his head down so that just the four tines on his left side are showing, nothing more than tiny glints of sunlight 200 yards off. We sit some more. I'm lying on my side and it's getting wet, the last of the snowmelt still pooled on the ground. Just then, Alyssa says, "They're getting up!" She has had to shift slightly, causing the bill of her blaze orange cap to slide over her eyes. When she adjusts it, she can no longer find the buck. And the sun, lower now, is lined up almost directly behind the four standing deer. "I can't see them," she says, and her voice is plaintive and desperate. Bruce repositions her hat a second time to cut down on the glare and points in the direction of the deer, which he and I can see clearly. "I still don't have them," Alyssa moans. "Keep looking, honey," Bruce says soothingly. The barrel of the rifle is waggling. She is way off now.

I'm worried. I'm worried that she'll acquire the wrong buck when she does get back on them because, once again, the smaller buck is standing in a more open spot. I'm worried that she'll rush the shot and miss or, worse, wound the buck and then we'll be in for a nighttime tracking job to find him before the coyotes do. Finally Alyssa says she can see the buck. I'm hoping it's the right one. I'm hoping he's standing broadside and still with his head down grazing so she doesn't get transfixed by the antlers. Bruce tells her to shoot now but she doesn't. I know she doesn't have a very solid platform, my coat and her shoulder, her body sitting atop her one folded-under knee, surely numb and cold by now. The longer she waits, the less confident I am that it will happen the way it ought to. After an eternity, during which I stay mum, prone, and praying, there comes the sharp, loud crack of the rifle. I had forgotten about the muzzle brake to reduce recoil on a girl's shoulder. Bruce explodes upward like a rocket. "You got him! You got him!" I rise in time to see the buck stagger and collapse. Bruce has lifted Alyssa and is hugging her. Then he hugs me. Then I hug Alyssa. Her dad and Erika, who've crept closer behind us, are shouting and coming up. "Run over there and make sure he's done," Bruce tells me. "I'll bring Alyssa." I take off, my own legs scarcely obeying me after being stuck so long in one position.

The buck is lying dead with his eyes open and a small hole in the middle of his body right behind the front leg. It is a perfect shot, the diagram any hunter has seen countless times of where to shoot a deer. The buck has a dark, forked 4×4 rack and is enormous, bigger than any whitetail I've ever seen, girthed up from months of feeding in anticipation of the rut. Alyssa swings her way over to pose for photos and get congratulatory first, second, and third hugs from everybody. The men, all three of us, are now looking away, drying the tears we would swear are just from the wind in our eyes. Bruce begins gutting the animal and has Alyssa take part, both their hands on his heavy knife as they slice up the belly. He removes the heart and hoists it for us to see. The top of it has been pulverized by the shot. "Can't shoot them any better'n this," he says. Alyssa strokes the flank of the buck quietly.

That night, after a celebratory dinner in Bruce's camper trailer, he prints out some of the shots he took on a digital printer. Everyone wants signed copies of Alyssa and Bruce together. She has her hands on the buck's antlers, striped in their own shadows by the slanting sun, the wind pushing both ends of Bruce's long mustache toward Alyssa. Alyssa signs all of hers with her name and "the deer slayer."

I tell her I can't get over the shot, that it is almost unbelievable. "Tell you something else," says Bruce. "It was actually 223 yards. I told her 200 because I didn't want her to overthink it or hold high or anything like that." I look at her and blurt, "You couldn't make that shot twice." I don't know why I say this, and even as the words come out of my mouth, I know they're stupid and just hope that she doesn't take offense. But the luminous girl with two earrings in her right ear and the Vermeer skin just regards me with that look, at once open and impenetrable, and says quietly, "I could make that shot again." She says this neither in irritation nor as a boast. It is just the truth, a thing that she knows. And she has never found there to be any great virtue in hiding the truth. It is at this moment that I see the steel beneath the beauty. Suddenly I understand. This is a girl who cannot be defeated, even if she should die in the fight. Of course she could make that same shot tomorrow. She could absolutely make that shot.

•

The Cuban Classic

I came to Cuba after hearing a number of things too interesting to ignore. One is that there are serious bass anglers and some big fish down here. The other is that the national tournament is almost exactly like the Bassmaster Classic except for a few details. Instead of having $50,000 rocket sleds, the anglers fish from rowboats. All fishing is catch-and-kill. (Protein is relatively hard to come by in Cuba, and the idea of returning it to the water has not even gotten off the ground yet. The fish go to either the anglers themselves or the Cuban Federation of Sport Fishing folks who work the competition.) And instead of the winner's getting half a million bucks — and many times that in endorsements and appearance fees — the top angler and team take home nothing more than a rinky-dink plastic trophy and bragging rights to being the best bass fishermen in the country.

I am more than a bit nervous on the 500-mile drive across a good chunk of the country from Havana to Bayamo. The guys I'm going to meet are fellow bass anglers, of course. But they are also Cuban. I, on the other hand, am a citizen of *El Empirio* — as they refer to their northern neighbor — the most powerful country on earth.

As we enter the city and my anxiety about meeting the 32 anglers competing in the Cuban national bass tournament rises, I tell my guide and translator, Samuel Yera, to stop at a gas station so I can arm myself with the one thing that bridges all socioeconomic barriers — beer. Samuel is a three-time tournament winner who failed to qualify this year because he spent too much time guiding saltwater clients for tarpon (which is why he is available to guide and translate for me). Ready with packs of cold Bucanero Fuerte, we park at the government dormitory by the local baseball stadium and head upstairs, guided by the sound of men's voices spilling out of an open door.

Meet the Champions

"Sam-well!" calls a man sitting on his bunk when he catches sight of my host. A burly shirtless guy with a farmer's tan, still dripping from a shower, he waddles over to embrace Yera. The men are sitting in the room, passing around a bottle of rum. Everyone crowds about their old friend, who is regarded as perhaps the most knowledgeable bass fisherman in Cuba.

He introduces me all around, and I shake hard, calloused hands. They are carpenters, security guards, and paper-mill workers. One is a local plastic surgeon, another a railroad engineer, another an artist. Special passes from the government allow them to be absent from work for the tournament. American anglers ready themselves for competition by studying the lake and fine-tuning their GPS settings. These guys have been strengthening their legs, backs, and especially their hands. The last thing the men want is blisters or fatigue slowing them down as they row to and from a spot that might hold a kicker fish on the three-bass stringer that each will weigh in.

I pass out beer and survey the room: eight beds with about 2 feet of hanger space in between, a bathroom off the end, a tiny porch outside. Some men have two rods, some just one, plus a little tackle box of some sort and, neatly ironed, the shirt and pants they will wear on the water. Some have an everyday ball cap and a special one with a fish on it for tournament finery. It strikes me that these guys, the top bass anglers in Cuba, have less gear than an average 10-year-old boy in the States.

Samuel is soon lost to me, deep in rapid conversation with a knot of anglers. They don't speak English and I don't *habla español,* but through smiles and gestures we find ways to communicate. One of the younger guys, with curly black hair and a Red Sox cap, motions me over to show off the plastic worms that he, like many others, makes himself. He uses dental clay to shape a mold of the bait to be copied, then melts down old lures, scrap plastic, whatever he can find. He mixes that with some kind of oil, heats it, and pours it into the mold. The result is a worm that looks surprisingly true to the original, right down to the faint Power Bait lettering on the tail.

The 9-inch black worm he displays has a few flecks of rubber where it shouldn't, but it will certainly catch fish. My new friend with the handmade worms is curious about something. Through Samuel, he asks my opinion: Do I prefer the Mann's Augertail worm to that company's Jelly worm? The Augertail has more flutter, of course, but sometimes the subtler action of the Jelly worm is better in heavy cover. I interrupt the translation to throw my hands up in despair. "Who the hell knows!" I find myself nearly shouting. I feel as if I've stumbled into some inverted reality — Alice in Bassland. "Besides, you know more about American baits than I do!" I take an equilibrium-restoring swig of the rum.

There Has Been a Small Change

Samuel informs me that there has been a change for tomorrow. The government promised 16 rowboats for the tournament but has delivered only 8. So the two-day event will now run over four days, the field alternating until everybody gets two full days on the water. In the United States, this would have provoked charges that the tournament was no longer fair. Not least among the reasons: An approaching cold front promises a difficult bite for whoever is on the water when it arrives.

But we are not in the United States, and so four days it will be. Actually, rowboats are quite a luxury, according to Samuel. "Most of our tournaments are done either wading or fishing from inner tubes."

Some of the men, he tells me, are market fishermen. They rise before dawn to bicycle to local lakes, spending all day kicking around the water. Eight or ten hours later, they deflate their tubes and ride home carrying rod, tackle, fins, tube, and their catch. This sounds like it would be fun for a while. To do it day after day, to *have* to do it, might not be.

I look around the room and notice the oars in the corners. For this, the national championship, each team has to bring their own. One set with aluminum shafts leans against the wall, but the others are completely homemade, poles with splits of roughly shaped wood nailed or screwed to the shafts. Two pairs sport blades of corrugated aluminum, a common roofing material, that has been hammered more or less flat.

The mood in the room is relaxed and happy. Tomorrow, on the water, they will compete. But for now they are celebrating having made the cut and seeing old friends. Samuel says there are about 80,000 members of the Cuban Federation of Sport Fishing, the organization that sponsors tournaments, of which number he believes 30,000 are bass anglers.

"But this is the most important tournament in Cuba, because we believe bass are the hardest fish, the most sporting. It's a big honor to the winner." The tournament began in 1969, and this is the 25th time it has been held on Lake Leonero in rural Granma province. When the rum reaches me again, I take another swig, grimace, and pretend to suffer mild convulsions. "Ah," I finally gasp. *"Que bueno!"* They laugh. Maybe I'm okay after all.

Some of the rods, I notice, are rigged with neon-bright orange or yellow line. I ask Samuel if the bright line doesn't spook fish. "You don't understand," he says, smiling. "Here there is no learning curve. The first time a fish gets caught is also the last time." One guy suddenly discovers something beneath his bed and holds it up with a cry of exclamation. It's a coconut shell filled with flowers, bird feathers, colored stones, and a tangle of old fishing line. *"Santeria!"* he announces — the Cuban folk religion that blends Christianity and African animistic beliefs, including the power of charms and spirits. Someone has put it there to jinx him. He deadpans that his skill is such that he will defy witchcraft. The room erupts in loud, friendly derision.

Not Your Average Yanqui Bass Tournament

Samuel and I seem to be doing an odd little dance. The deal is that I hold up lures for his inspection and he keeps shaking his head. He negates a 4-3D 8-inch jointed Rapala. He turns down a 6-inch bubblegum floating worm. "Bigger," he says. We're in a motorized skiff on Lake Leonero. The anglers, two-man teams from Cuba's 14 provinces (plus an extra team from the host province and one from the Island of Youth, off Cuba's southern coast), are spread out over the lake somewhere around us.

I'm here to watch the fishermen, but Samuel says we need to keep our distance from them, especially on the first day. "The fish and the anglers are both very sensitive to noise." This, I am pretty sure, is bull. I think Samuel just wants to catch some fish, partly to ease his obvious chagrin at not being in the race, and partly because he is just a diehard bass man.

And the bass on Leonero like their baits not only big but apparently disruptive, too, because the lure that finally gets the nod is a no-name Devil's Horse-style topwater. This fat cigar of a bait has propellers fore and aft, and treble hooks the size of little chandeliers. It's so big and raucous that I've never even been tempted to tie it on. But Samuel likes it.

"Now you're speaking," he says. I ask why the fish here prefer big lures and whether that is the case all over Cuba. "It's not," he replies. "Some places you need small lures. And I don't even know the reason they prefer the big lures on this lake. They just do."

The morning is calm; a light wind ripples the water. Using Samuel's baitcasting reel and a 6-foot rod, I cast and retrieve. The lure is wiggling like some hyperactive dachshund that fell off the dock when a bass engulfs it. It disappears in a sudden sinkhole of water and I set the hook, the fish diving, pulling left, heading for the pads. I turn it and bring it in. It's the gamest 2-pounder I've ever tangled with — fat, healthy, and thoroughly ticked off at having a hook in its mouth. Samuel is casting a large Zara Spook on a big spinning rod, and soon both of us are catching fish every second or third cast, a number of which run 3 pounds.

It's crazy-good video-game fishing, the flat-out most sustained largemouth action I've ever had. After about 10 minutes of this, Samuel stows his rod. "No good here," he says. I ignore him, cast again, and ask if he'd mind explaining just what the Sam Hill he's talking about. "Place like this, you can wear your arm out. But you can't win a tournament."

What, I ask, would it take to win?

"Here? You need an average of 5 pounds

each fish to be competitive. To win, it usually takes an average of 6 pounds, maybe a little more." I look at him. He's smiling but he's not kidding.

We need to invade this country.

Having Fun

We move the boat. It is January, and the females are getting ready to spawn, Samuel says. He is looking for a certain water color that he says the bass prefer. "Where it is coffee-colored — you see over there? — you will not find fish. And often the big females nest in the open water, away from the pads. Often they like green hydrilla flats. If you are just fishing the structure you see, you will not get them."

We keep moving.

At last he anchors near a big flat off a channel. On my fourth cast, something smashes my lure. "Big bass!" Samuel says. "Big bass!" It bends my short baitcasting rod nearly double before I get it to the boat. It has a mouth like a trash can. Samuel says it's a 7-pounder. That would make it the second-biggest bass of my life. I catch two 5-pounders over the next 15 minutes.

"Having fun?" asks Samuel.

On the way back to the put-in, we cruise by some of the competitors. Most are scat-

tered over a single area, a large bowl surrounded by endless pads. One boat, however, is off by itself, fishing a more distant
edge of lily pads. It's the team from Las
Tunas, a neighboring province, an experienced duo that is expected to do well here.
The guy at the oars stops when he sees us,
calls to Samuel, stands, and struggles to
hoist a stringer that's so heavy it's all he can
do to lift it clear of the water. There are
about 10 fish on it, big oblong bass. One
will go nearly 10 pounds, another just over
7.

In the United States, you no longer see
such a sight. That's a good thing, of course.
Any lake would get fished out fast if it were
subject to a sustained harvest of its biggest
bass. On the other hand, it's something to
behold. The guys will winnow the catch
down to six, three per angler. The biggest
looks to be a 10-pounder. There are two
others that will go close to 7.

The Las Tunas guys tell Samuel that they
lost two big fish, one of which would have
gone 10, when the line got tangled up with
the anchor rope. They have caught virtually
all their fish on big worms. And they are
fishing them in a way I've never seen.

The guy in the bow has a 9- or 10-inch
dark worm Texas-rigged on what looks to

be a 3/0 offset worm hook with about a 1D 8-ounce sinker. He has a 7-foot spinning rod, which he uses to throw the worm as far as he can. Then he reels it steadily back, just like a crankbait. On his fourth cast, he suddenly stops reeling at what must be a strike of some kind. He pauses for just a second, lowers the rod, reels in slack, then sets the hook hard. His line begins to dance, and soon he is boating another 5- or 6-pound fish.

I have Samuel ask him what the take is like. "Just the sensation of weight, or maybe a tap," he translates. "Nothing strong. They inhale it, not bite it. You give them a moment, take the slack, and hook them." The guy says they fish the worm higher or lower in the water column as conditions dictate. "We fish always this worm," one of them, Onix Hernandez, says. "If I see fish hitting the poppers of other fishermen, I just fish it closer to the surface." They never let it hit bottom and never stop reeling unless they feel a fish. I've never heard of crankbait-style worming. But many things, I'm learning, are different in Cuba. And it's awfully hard to argue with what works.

Back on shore, the boats are pulling in to the mud bank that is the landing area. Pigs and chickens run around, looking for any crumbs dropped from lunch bags. The Las Tunas team shows me its worms: all hand poured and rigged on homemade light football-type jigheads. Their fish are still on the stringer in the water. Most of the fishermen are playing it close to the vest, keeping their stringers submerged. This is partly to keep the fish wet as long as possible — they won't be officially weighed here but back in Bayamo, a two-hour drive during which the fish will be out of water. And it's partly just to keep other teams guessing about how they did.

That afternoon, in a small square in the dusty city, the official weigh-in finally takes place on old-fashioned mechanical scales that might have been borrowed from a fruit stand. Moving away from the pack has paid off for Las Tunas. They are in first place with six fish weighing 38 pounds, more than 6 pounds ahead of the second-place team, Villa Clara, which has 31 pounds. One of the Granma anglers has his photo taken with a fish of just over 10 pounds, the biggest bass caught in a tournament on Leonero in years. The guys who didn't get to fish today look grave. Thirty-eight pounds is not unheard of, but it will be tough to equal, let alone surpass.

The Beauty of the Ugly Stik

On the second day — my last, since I had only expected to be here for a two-day tournament — Samuel once again takes me fishing because of his commendable wish not to disturb the other anglers. Once again, I'm using his baitcaster, while he uses the big spinning rod. I tried the latter for a couple of casts and disliked it. It's too big, too heavy, not particularly sensitive, and a lot of work to crank. He hefts the rod. "It's what every Cuban asks his family or friends in the States to bring him," he says. "Seven-foot medium-heavy Ugly Stik spinning rod with a Penn 7500 SS."

"Why?"

He hefts it again, working a topwater. "Durability," he says. "An Ugly Stik is like a '57 Chevrolet. Almost indestructible." I look at the Penn reel, all 25.5 ounces of it, with its measly three ball bearings. "A Cuban would take this over a Shimano or a Daiwa every time," he adds. "Very dependable. Goes forever. And easy to work on." He grunts, sets the hook, and pulls in a 5-pounder. "Time to move. Look for the big ones."

We don't find the big ones, but we do tire our arms out on the 2- to 4-pounders. And there are worse ways to spend a day. As we head back toward shore, we pass not too far from one of the two teams from Granma province. One evidently has a big fish on because he is excitedly telling his co-angler to get the net. But the net man lunges at the fish awkwardly, frightening it. The fish jumps close to the boat, and the line goes slack. Both men slump back to their seats, despairing at having lost what was obviously a huge bass. Samuel shakes his head in commiseration. "It's just because they're not used to boats, not used to nets. We don't carry nets when we wade or tube. That fish, it could have won them the tournament maybe."

It could have, but it didn't. A few days after I arrive back in the United States, I get an e-mail from Samuel. Las Tunas won the tournament with a two-day, 12-fish total of 78 pounds 8 ounces. Granma was just 5 ounces behind. The fifth-place team, he writes, from his home province of Villa Clara, should have finished in third place. "They had an 11- or 12-pound fish on a big Husky Jerk. But it made one last run by the boat and opened the treble hook and escaped."

On my last evening in Bayamo, I am once again sitting on the end of a bed drinking beer with the guys while a bottle of rum slowly laps the room. I have brought an entire duffel bag of plastics, lures, and line cadged from Yamamoto, Berkley, and Rapala. I dump it out on the floor and it vanishes in the time it takes a school of piranhas to clean a cow carcass. The only problem is that most of the plastics are tiny, 6 inches or less. No matter. Some anglers are even now squeezing the packs to gauge how well they will melt down to be recast into larger baits.

One of the guys from Granma can't even wait that long. He pulls a 4-inch Senko (green pumpkin) from its pack, studies it, hefts it experimentally. Then he cuts the first 3 inches off one of his 9-inch black worms with a knife, carefully heats both the cut tip of the worm and one end of the Senko with his lighter, and presses the two together until they cool. The result is a 10-inch, two-tone hybrid ribbon tail. He smiles, wiggles it seductively, lifts it for my inspection.

"Beel?" he asks. "What you think?" I give him a thumbs-up and a smile, already vowing never to throw away a chewed-up worm again.

"Oh, yeah. They'll clobber that thing."

■ ■ ■ ■

IV
HUNTING WITHOUT
PANTS:
AND OTHER
NECESSARY SKILLS

■ ■ ■ ■

THE DEER
NEXT DOOR

It's not that I was cocky at the start of last year's deer season. It's just that the only new equipment I expected to need was an Alum-i-Lite Game Cart from Cabela's to help me get my trophies out of the woods and into the record books without hurting my back.

My confidence came from having lucked into the mother of all honey holes behind the house of my new best friend, Jay Wheeler. Jay has the good sense to live where most monster deer can be found these days: the 'burbs. His backyard is essentially a wooded funnel that connects a municipal park being denuded by protected deer to one of the last cornfields in the county. (Developers have long been eyeing that cornfield, reasoning that town houses are a better crop than corn, which does little to support the global market for Tyvek house wrap.)

I spent much of last summer behind my binoculars watching deer move between the park and the corn. There were big tour groups of does, gangs of unruly 1- and 2-year-old bucks, and, just as the light gave out, a few old monsters. A couple of these looked to be genetic freaks, deer with swing sets exploding out of their skulls, antlers so heavy they had to hurt to lug around.

Jay is a big dude who flew helicopters in Vietnam and usually has an unlit La Gloria Cubana cigar in his mouth. He runs a successful consulting company and has a lovely wife, Vicki. He is a guy with either a big heart or a small brain, because all he asked in return for hunting privileges was that I not park on the grass. In fact, I would happily have repainted his house, cleaned the gutters, and prepared his taxes in perpetuity. He can't put his cars in the garage because both bays are crowded with racks from bucks he has taken from his backyard over the years. When I asked what time of year he starts hunting, he shrugged. "Oh, I usually just wait for the rut," he said.

As bow season opened in mid-September, I parked my new folding deer carrier in Jay's garage, half regretting that its shiny new finish would soon be marred by deer blood.

Hunting season is both a wonderful and a

dangerous time to be a freelance outdoor writer. It's wonderful because, as master of your own time, you don't need anyone's permission to blow off work and go hunting. On the other hand, it's dangerous because, as master of your own time, you don't need anyone's permission to blow off work and go hunting.

After carefully reviewing my dwindling monetary resources, I did what any diehard hunter would do. I turned off the answering machine, changed my e-mail setting from *available for hire* to *block anything that looks remotely business-related,* and began hunting my brains out. I was there at dawn. I was there at dusk. And it wasn't even October. I saw plenty of does and yearling bucks, but the big heads were scarce. Weeks later, in the honeyed light of a late-October afternoon, I finally drew on an 8-pointer standing broadside and oblivious as he fed on acorns 16 yards away. He was racked a tad wider than his ears, and anywhere else I'd have taken him in a heartbeat. But I wasn't anywhere else. I was here. Tine Town. Antler Alley. The Funnel of Fun.

A week later, one of those great heads appeared out of thin air 36 yards out, stretching his thick neck to sniff a rub. I slowly stood, drew, and tried to settle my 30-yard pin just over his back. Personally, I was fine. But my legs picked that moment to audition for the *Lord of the Dance.* The buck busted me in a heartbeat, then did that trick that only old survivors know: He didn't wheel, snort, or jump. He simply dissolved, like the Cheshire Cat — now-you-see-me-now-you-don't — leaving the outlines of his rack hanging in the air momentarily. I wished for nothing so much at that instant as the ability to kick my own butt.

By November, I was in the full throes of my addiction, hitting the woods each morning and losing whatever tenuous mental edge I might have had. Big bucks don't dawdle during the rut. More than one five-second window of opportunity opened and shut before I'd even realized what I was looking at.

On the morning of November 12, I showed up as usual, only to find Jay standing in my headlights with a grin. "Went out yesterday afternoon for the first time and got lucky. Arrowed a nice buck and gutted him, but I need a hand getting him out. You mind?" And then Jay and I went out and loaded one of those swing-set bucks on my cart. "Sure am glad you bought this thing," Jay said.

WHY MEN LOVE KNIVES

There's something about a good knife that speaks to you on a primal level. It's been this way for about 2 1/2 million years, ever since David E. Petzal was just a gleam in his papa's eye and some nameless hunter-gatherer first began pounding rocks together. Anthropologists say we first made tools for two purposes: pounding and cutting. Your pounding tool is simplicity itself; pretty much any rock will serve to crush a mastodon bone to get at the marrow. But you need something very specific — a sharp edge — to butcher an animal or scrape a hide. Imagine that first hominid flaking a piece of rock into a shaped edge that fit his paw. Imagine the delight in his face as he hefted it and discovered its powers. I bet you anything he smiled, elbowed the nearest guy, and showed off his creation. And the message — verbal or not — has remained unchanged from that day to this:

Got me a nice little cutting rock here. Check it out.

I understand this feeling in its totality. Not long ago, I picked up a very nice "rock" indeed. Mine was a serious folder, an Emerson CQC-7. It's more knife than anybody but a Special Operations guy could justify. But it's not more knife than I wanted. I liked the way it felt in my hand. The Teflon-coated blade is just over 3 inches long and partially serrated for cutting rope or other fibrous material. It has a Tanto point that can punch through steel. Its handle is an epoxy-fiberglass laminate known in the trade as G-10 that almost seems to adhere to your hand. The knife comes with a clip that positions it head-down in your pocket so that it's in the right position when you draw it, and there's a little round thumb plate affixed to the blade for one-handed opening. The click of the blade locking into position is authoritative. It's a sound that says, I can handle this.

The knife is pure function with no concession to appearance. Because of that, it is all the more beautiful. Like the Parthenon, there's not a truly straight line in it. It cost . . . let's just say, enough that you might be tempted to pay cash so your wife doesn't see the figure on the credit-card bill. You could easily field dress an elephant with this thing. Heck, you could probably build a house. It makes me feel more competent than I actually am. A good knife will do this to you.

The only problem is that it's sending me into a severe funk because there is nothing in my life that justifies a knife of this seriousness. I am not in the Special Forces. I am a middle-aged bald guy who lives in the suburbs with a wife and two kids, a big mortgage, and a 1991 Honda Civic. Last night, with my new knife in my pocket, my younger daughter and I fell asleep in her bed after reading *The Poky Little Puppy.* And not long ago, an attractive young woman held the door for me as I entered a store behind her. When I thanked her, she said, "You're welcome, sir." That "sir" said things that no man who still has his own teeth and knees should have to hear.

So maybe my acquiring this knife is a reminder to myself that beneath this veneer of normalcy there still lives a hunter-gatherer whose every day is a struggle against a world filled with sudden and unforeseen dangers. True, saber-toothed cats no longer tread in the night, waiting to pounce, but there are challenges nonetheless. Just last week, for example, I was setting out the garbage cans at the end of the driveway when I ran into my neighbor Dave, who was doing the same. Dave is about my age and is suffering from the effects of having recently traded in a sweet little pocket-rocket convertible for a green minivan. There we were, two housebroken hominids with lawns full of dandelions, wrangling our garbage cans. Then Dave began stomping the cardboard box from a new baby gate, as the trash guys won't pick up any container that hasn't been flattened to under 6 inches. He was kicking it harder and harder, to little effect, when I said, "Let me give you a hand." I slid my knife out of my pants pocket, and the blade clicked into place. With four quick strokes, I slit the cardboard seams. The box collapsed.

"Whoa," said Dave. "That is one serious little blade."

"Yeah," I said proudly, offering it handle-first. "Check it out."

PITY THE FOOL

I never expected to say this, but here goes: I'm glad the season is almost over. I say this for the following reasons.

If, like me, you are fool enough to dream of killing a monstrous whitetail buck with a pointy stick, the state where I hunt guarantees your right to have at it from mid-September to the bitter end of January. And until the season runs out and hunters still afield are subject to prosecution, this is exactly what I intend to do, even though on a cold January afternoon I am about as likely to see Jesus wandering around during daylight hours as a deer.

During a lunch meeting with my boss (me) back in August, we drafted a memorandum of understanding stating that the company would adopt a liberal leave policy during hunting season for all staff (me). It turns out that revenue can take a substantial hit when the corporate goal is "earn enough for gas money for the next three months." Especially in this global economy.

I seem to be aging rapidly. The circles under my eyes are developing circles of their own. I am experiencing frequent bouts of blurred vision, forgetfulness, and confusion as to my whereabouts at any given moment. So this is how it feels to be David E. Petzal on a good day.

Failing to get a reaction from me with standard by-mail death threats, the Book-of-the-Month Club has hired a bounty hunter to find me.

The guy who holds down the midnight shift at my local 7-Eleven rings me up for a 32-ounce coffee and an Artery Buster Biscuit even before I place the cellophane bag of death in the microwave. He may do this simply to be helpful; he may do it to minimize the time the wild-eyed guy wearing camo pants and an untucked pajama shirt spends in the store.

The 1-ounce amber bottles currently rolling around under the seats in my car are making such loud clinking sounds that the entire family now refuses to ride in it. They have also made complaints about the perfume, which I would describe as a bracing blend of single-doe estrous, Trail's End #307, and intruder-buck scent.

After two hours on stand without seeing any deer, I start to think I'd be warmer if I could just take a glass of ice water and pour it down my pants.

Last week, after sitting quietly in a cafe for 10 minutes, I tried to rattle up a waiter using two spoons.

When I happen to cross paths with my wife, Jane, from time to time, she reminds me that insanity is continuing to do the same thing but expecting different results.

Now that the season is nearly over, I am almost looking forward to the traditional promises to family and collection agencies to do better. I pledge to be a better husband, father, and provider to Jane and . . . I believe our baby's name is Emma.

Oh, right. And Jane says she's not a baby any more, she's almost 5. In fact, my wife is holding up a calendar at this very moment and indicating that Emma's birthday is in six days. And what she wants more than anything else is a 1997 Pink Splendor Barbie that retails for $900. Right now, I'm not in a position to haggle. Pink Splendor Barbie it is. (Note to self: Have bow appraised for cash value immediately.)

What should a man think about at such trying moments? Me, I go for deer every time. I find it soothing to meditate on the bucks that have survived the season and are even now walking around out there in the dark. Bucks whose antlers have already begun to loosen ever so slightly. In just four or five months, performing a trick whose power is undiminished by the millennia, those deer will start to grow new, larger ones. Almost before you know it, hunting season will be upon us again. And the corporate goal of Bill Heavey Freelance Enterprises Ltd. will once again be reduced to two words: gas money.

THE PSYCHO SEASON

March is that magical month when Nature, rolling over in response to the sportsman's gentle nudge, glares back with a party girl's bloodshot eyes and tells you to stick it in your ear. Rebuffed, you stare out onto a soggy landscape in which it is impossible to tell where the earth stops and the sky begins. That's when it hits you. It's nuclear winter, that part of the year when all life seems to pause, and darkness and extreme cold envelop the earth. You'd see more activity inside the brain of a fundamentalist preacher.

The ducks and geese are south of the border, sucking on a cold *cerveza* and stubbing their webbed feet into the warm sand. Surviving deer are thicketed up, still hearing the whistle of rounds that grazed their briskets. More than one grizzled 8-pointer is even now shaking his head in disbelief. "Chasing does during daylight in a bean-field? Why not just stand in the middle of an Izaak Walton shooting range and get it over with?" He murmurs thanks to the trinity that has been saving his kind since 1963: (1) the .300 Winchester Magnum rifle; (2) the got-me-more-gun-than-you hunters from New York to Texas who choose this firearm because you never know when a seriously lost bull elk or marauding grizzly could pop up three farms over; and (3) the shooter's flinch that happens when you combine (1) and (2). Without them, that buck would be swimming in tomato sauce and pinto beans right now.

So what are your choices? Spring gobbler season is 30 days — one eternity — from now. Pattern your gun. Practice your purrs, cutts, and yelps. Lather, rinse, repeat until insane. Psych wards are full of superb turkey callers.

Fishing? Absolutely. Let me offer some tips. Jig a 1-ounce spoon vertically in deep water and use a Carolina-rigged finesse worm for shallow presentations. Because a bass only needs to eat about once every two weeks when the water is below 50 degrees, your odds of getting a bite are about equal to those of having Donald Trump become your apprentice. But these are still the lures to use: the jig because you won't wear yourself out casting the damn thing, and the worm because it's a good "indicator" lure. Any subtle tick in your line could, theoretically, be a bass. More likely, you have lost control of your hand muscles, indicating the onset of hypothermia. As always, you owe it to your loved ones to wear a PFD while on the water — but not because it will save your life. Fall in and the shock of the cold water will instantly render you incapable of movement. By having the foresight to freeze upright, bobbing next to your boat, you spare search-and-rescue crews untold hours with the grappling hook. And the minnows will not have a chance to nibble your face into hamburger, giving the mortician something to work with should your heirs opt for an open casket.

My advice for this time of year, if you are gainfully employed, is to bank some serious overtime pay against future outings. As an outdoor writer, I don't have this option. When there's nothing going on outside, there's not much going on upstairs. What do I do with such freedom? Mostly I sit in my basement, stewing in frustration and the long underwear I haven't changed in two days and a beard I haven't shaved in three, drinking coffee until I start speaking in tongues.

Last year, after several days of this, I couldn't take it anymore. I put on my new Filson Wetlands Hunting Hat (purchased during a particularly severe bout of cabin fever), buckled it under my chin, and ran into my yard. Using only a pocketknife and a shoelace, I tried to fashion a bow drill, a friction-based fire starter I'd made exactly once in a survival course. I started by attacking a dead cedar tree. Soon I had fashioned the bow, spindle, socket, and fireboard. I spent the next three hours on one knee, bent over a wet piece of wood, trying to start a fire. In the process I cut my hand deeply and thoroughly muddied my long johns. But the experience brought home two important lessons. One is to never go into the woods without NATO-rated waterproof matches, a flint and steel, and a good lighter. The other is that it takes one heck of a long time for winter to turn into spring, and there's not a lot you can do about it.

So if you happen to see an unshaven guy outside in his underwear, talking to himself and wearing a camouflage hat, just smile and wave as if it's the most natural thing in the world. Which, in a way, it is.

THE BLIND-HOG
JACKPOT

Once or twice a year, some manufacturer of hunting gear mistakes me for a serious outdoor writer and invites me on a free hunt. Since the call usually comes two days before the event, I am obviously not their first choice. But if Philip Bourjaily suddenly has a custom shotgun fitting or David E. Petzal needs his back waxed for a *Hot Shots of the Gun World* photo shoot, they may call me. As a writer whose only tangible asset is his reputation, I have a strict policy for dealing with all such offers. I accept immediately.

The people arranging this one were the manufacturers of Gore-Tex fabrics and Scent-Lok hunting duds, products that rank right up there with the pyramids and Britney Spears as among the greatest creations in history. They invited me to a two-and-a-half-day whitetail hunt on the 20,000-acre Halff Brothers Ranch in south Texas. The bad news was that it was for "management" bucks, the small deer that are periodically removed from the herd. The good news was that in south Texas these are gargantuan, bigger than 99 percent of the deer a typical hunter sees in his lifetime.

On a short hunt, it's important to start botching things up early. At the airport, I was unable to lock my bow case because I had left the key on the kitchen table. "You don't lock it, you don't take it," the security guy said. Every pore in my body opened and began to leak sweat. I was saved by Eric Eshleman, a TSA screener who fills his downtime on the job by picking luggage locks. He locked the case using a twisted paper clip, then sent me on my way with the new key. I hereby nominate him as the permanent head of Homeland Security.

I didn't mess up again for nearly 20 hours. But bright and early the next morning, I decided to leave my release in the truck when guide Greg Bladgett and I were dropped off. We sat in a pop-up blind, as lethal as lawn jockeys, while a high-racked 7-pointer fed contentedly just yards away. Greg and I must be related, because he had decided to leave his cell phone in the truck, so we couldn't call anyone to bring the release back. After a long silence, he dribbled tobacco juice in the dirt and whispered, "Aren't we a couple of gold-plated idjits?"

On the final morning, with my chances to get a deer running out, Greg saw me readying my bow and said, "Ain't gonna need that today." As I hadn't rezeroed my rifle, he handed me his bull-barreled 7mm mag, equipped with a 4×12 scope, and a handful of 140-grain ballistic-tip handloads. We set up in the dark, prone behind a log looking straight down at least 400 yards of road. At dawn, five does emerged to feed. Ten minutes later, I put the crosshairs on the shoulder of a shooter buck and squeezed. When the smoke cleared, Greg turned red. "You shot the wrong buck!" he hissed. Then he turned pale. "I'm going to get fired." I had shot the only buck I had seen, which had since vanished. Better — or worse — much farther down the road lay a second, larger buck in its final throes.

Greg told me he had seen the second buck just before I fired, knew it was too big, and figured it wouldn't make any difference on the shot of the deer we had agreed I would take. Greg thought the deer I'd aimed at did not react as if it had been hit. I was pretty sure I'd made a good shot.

Together, we walked down the road. At 120 yards, the animal I'd aimed for lay 15 feet off the road, as dead as a rock. He was a big, beautiful 130-class eight. We walked another 130 steps to the second buck. Evidently the bullet had continued on and hit it in the spine and femoral artery. He was definitely out of my price range — a 150-class trophy with 9 points, tons of mass, and kickers galore. Depending on how you chose to look at it, I had made either the shot or the screwup of a lifetime. Greg called his boss, who in turn called the ranch manager and biologist. "Don't you touch a thing," he said to me. "I'm gonna show them exactly how it happened."

Many conferences in closed truck cabs later, Greg was cleared. The county limit is two bucks, so that wasn't a problem at all. In the end, the ranch manager decided that I could keep the buck I'd shot at. The second will be on display this fall in the lodge of the Halff Brothers Ranch. They took my photo holding both bucks — more antler than I'd cumulatively killed in my lifetime, looking exactly like what I was, a no-name hunter who'd just hit the blind-hog jackpot. And I just want to say that I couldn't have done it without my Gore-Tex and Scent-Lok clothing. It is absolutely the best.

OUT OF MY LEAGUE

Money can't buy happiness, but it can substantially upgrade the quality of your misery. Take me, for example. It's a crisp morning in southwest Georgia, and I'm holding a slim Italian-made 20-gauge at port arms as I stride through the brush. The engraving of quail and dogs on it cost the eyesight of untold craftsmen, and the Circassian walnut stock has a grain like a Damascus blade, flashing purple highlights when the sun hits it. A hundred yards ahead, past the wire grass and plots of milo and sunflower, I can make out the well-muscled haunches of English pointers that receive more daily attention than those of Jennifer Lopez.

Suddenly, the dogs turn to marble. Jack, Thommy, and I pull even with each other. Jack Unruh, whom I had never met before, is the illustrator whose depictions of me as a clueless nimrod on the back page of *Field*

& Stream magazine have brought squeals of joy from my daughters. We arranged to meet in Georgia so I could finally confront him about this, man to man. But he disarmed me by sneaking up on me at the baggage carousel at the airport and whispering, "You're even uglier in real life." Thommy is a friend of Jack's from way back. He owns about 9 billion acres of land managed exclusively for wild quail, and I am looking for the right moment to tell him that I want to be his new best friend.

We pause, awaiting Thommy's nod, then advance. The birds erupt — always the same, yet always startling — and scatter like jazz musicians, each riffing wildly on the theme of "downwind and fast." Jack is a pretty good shot. Armed with this self-pointing stick, even I make a pretty sight every so often. But Thommy, toting a .410 soda straw (albeit a Purdey), plucks them down with a single-mindedness that Old Scratch himself would admire. He is the best shot I have ever seen. After a while, even the .410 seems like too much gun.

Growing conditions below the Mason-Dixon Line are especially suited to larger-than-life characters like Thommy, who combines scandalous amounts of old money and charm, plenty of horsepower upstairs, and a hint of insanity from having been on the losing side in the Civil War (don't take this the wrong way; it runs in my own family).

"My ancestors were quite successful raising cotton and tobacco, and Daddy did the same in peanuts," he tells me while we rotate in a fresh pair of dogs. "But my personal cash flow improved dramatically upon my father's death, when I was 19." Thommy's father, a flinty fellow who could afford any gun on earth, hunted with a battered Remington Model 11 with a Cutt's compensator. Fancy guns were for fools. You showed your respect for the birds with your shooting ability. His pleasure must have been keen when his only son took to quail hunting right out of the box. Thommy shot his first limit by age 9 and was a nationally ranked skeet shooter as a teen. He knew without being told to conceal his yearning for fancy firearms.

"There are people around here who will tell you that I ordered my first Purdey before my father was in his grave. Not so. It was the Monday morning *after* the service. At which time I ordered three.

"I knew Daddy wouldn't have approved, and I regret that. In fairness to myself, however, he had his own secrets. One was that his grandfather had come to Georgia to escape hanging for horse thievery in Virginia. Another was that I am actually the child of a woman he met only once and sent off to New Orleans with a trust fund." Although this seemed quite a confession, it was clear Thommy wasn't telling me anything he hadn't told many others. And you don't really talk to men like Thommy. You listen, nodding in the appropriate places.

I made a double late in the hunt, a sensation so sweet that I wanted nothing so much at that moment as the financial wherewithal to experience it regularly. But time moves fast in Fat City, especially with a shot like Thommy. We had our limit by early afternoon, and he left soon after, driving north to check out a promising dog.

Jack and I drove back to our motel, where I found the smell of Lysol unexpectedly welcome, returning me to a world I recognized. We cleaned the birds outside and iced a dozen. The remaining 12 we dredged in flour and pan-fried in the kitchenette. We sat on the parking-lot curb just outside our room, the grease spot on the paper towel between us spreading as the birds disappeared. Sipping pricey bird-trip Scotch from paper cups, we watched the red sun slip into the slotted horizon. I found myself envying Thommy, yet relieved to be back from cloud nine. "You know what it is?" I said to Jack. "I'm too screwed up to have that much money. I couldn't handle it."

Jack sipped his whiskey and smiled. "Aw, don't worry. I don't think it's going to happen." We touched paper cups and drank again. Then, realizing I'd just been insulted, I leaned over and took the last bird for myself.

En Garde!

Recently, the editor in chief of *Field & Stream,* Sid Evans, invited me to chase tarpon and snook with him in Florida. I accepted enthusiastically and began sweating like a low-level mafioso asked to go for a boat ride. Possible reasons for the summons include the following: (1) He has just read one of my expense reports a little too closely, (2) David E. Petzal is again lobbying for me to cover carp noodling in North Korea, or, worst of all, (3) he expects me to fly-fish. In which case I am toast. On the off chance that years of neglect have improved my casting skills, I get out my fly rod, set up in the backyard, and begin hitting myself in the forehead with a weighted nymph.

It's not that I don't know how to fly-fish. In just 25 years, I have gone from raw beginner to advanced beginner. But here's the thing: I have almost always felt like a hypocrite with a fly rod in hand, as if I were trying to impress somebody watching from the bushes. And I've always despised the snobbery of so many fly-fishermen. Plus, I stink at it.

I can hear you long-rod boys getting your backs up already. "We're not better, just different," you huff. "After all, what really matters is having a good time." Translation: "Our idea of entertainment is Shakespeare, and yours is the back of a Froot Loops box. But the important thing is that we both love to read."

My idea of fun is catching fish. Tons of them if possible. I love the tug and the way all three of us — the fish, the line, and I — become electrically connected for a few moments. I can count on zero fingers the number of times I've gone to bed thinking, *Damn, that would have been a pretty good day if I hadn't caught so many fish.* But you can't tell a fly-fisherman that. He'll give you some mumbo jumbo about "loving the process," spit white wine in your eye, and run you over with his Saab.

Despair over the outing with Sid drives me to set up a casting lesson with fly-fishing legend Lefty Kreh a couple of days before the trip. Nervous as a fat hog in December,

I call that morning to confirm the appointment.

"What time did I tell you?" Lefty asks.

"Eleven," I say. "Don't you remember?"

"Hell, I'm 80 years old," he cackles. "I don't even remember why I just came upstairs." Put a fly rod in Lefty's hands, however, and he remembers everything. We get right to it, casting on a pond near his house. "Forget all that crap about the clock face," he tells me. "It's not where you start or end, but what direction the rod tip is traveling when you stop that determines where your cast will go. And it sure ain't about power. I can throw a line 100 feet into the wind with two fingers." Holding the rod between his thumb and first finger, he does exactly that. It's like having Harry Houdini tell you how easy it is to pick locks with your toes or Dan Marino explain that any newborn could throw a perfect spiral 70 yards.

In spite of myself, I begin to make progress. "That's it," says Lefty. "Firm wrist. And forget that B.S. about holding the elbow in tight. It can move all you want as long as you keep it on the same level. Imagine your elbow sliding along a shelf. Yeah!" For a few minutes there, I actually believe I can pull it off.

In the Everglades three days later, I am offered a chance to take the bow platform and cast a big fly tight into the mangroves for snook. I confess to not being a great fly caster.

After watching me for a few minutes, our guide quietly begins to assemble some spinning tackle and hands the long rod to Sid. I am delighted to report that he is not the world's most stylish caster, but he does possess an annoying knack of getting the fly to land where he wants it to go. Possibly it is just afraid of becoming unemployed otherwise. Anyway, it wasn't long before he had a good snook on. And a minute later, I had one, too.

That night over dinner, the guide announced that he'd had a cancellation the next day and that he and his brother would be going out to smack a few snook themselves.

"Fly rods?" I asked.

"Hell, no," he retorted, taking a long pull on his beer. "Not when I'm trying to get one for the grill."

Long story short, my editor doesn't care about my fly-fishing skills, and I still have a job. At least until he invites me to go skeet shooting with him.

GIRL MEETS BLUEGILL

The first rule of introducing a kid to fishing is that you absolutely must catch fish. Later on, he or she may be open to the idea of "enjoying the experience." But at 5, believe me, they are out for blood. You get two, maybe three shots before even the dumbest *Clifford the Big Red Dog* DVD beats the hell out of watching a bobber do nothing. And then you have lost your child to all sorts of horrors: gangs, methamphetamines, violin lessons.

The first time I take Emma fishing, she is psyched right up until she steps into the canoe. Normally, water holds no terror for her. But now, just as we are about to shove off, her lower lip starts to tremble. "Gustave," she whispers.

Gustave is an all-too-real Nile crocodile we have recently seen on a National Geographic special. He is more than 20 feet long and in the past few decades has eaten

307

over 200 people, mostly fishermen in a river near Lake Tanganyika. The story of the French naturalist trying to trap Gustave for study made for a riveting documentary. The only problem was that he failed. Gustave is still out there.

"Don't worry, Monk-a-lula," I tell Emma. "Gustave never comes here. It's too cold." Emma checks the shoreline for crocs. I can almost see the machinery in her brain weighing her father's perfect record (so far) of keeping her safe versus the primordial reptilian monster. The first tear streaks her cheek. Game over.

The second time, I decide to fish from shore. Emma has already shown remarkable casting potential with her little Tigger-themed push-button outfit, recently putting so much wrist into a cast with the yellow "fishy" practice plug that she snapped the line. I bait a No. 6 Eagle Claw hook with a worm just below the bobber. Emma attempts three casts, none of which reach the water. I gently take over, but the rig is so light that even I can barely get it out there. Fishless after two minutes, she starts throwing gravel into the water. "Monk, that scares the fish," I tell her.

"That's okay," she assures me brightly. I change locations, wanting at least to produce a fish so she understands the goal here. She follows, with larger handfuls of gravel.

"I'm fishing here," I say. There is a silence. "Can we go home?" she asks. Zero for two.

It's the bottom of the ninth inning. Unless we get on fish quickly the next time, my daughter will be lost to me forever. She will become an animal rights activist and be trampled to death by hogs while attempting to liberate the stockyard at a Jimmy Dean plant.

The day of reckoning finds us at a shallow bass pond. I am prepared with two Shimano kids' outfits (one for backup), a bucket of minnows, juice boxes, string cheese, SPF 50 sunblock, insect repellent, and spare underwear. Emma works up the nerve to stick her hand in the bait bucket. When a minnow brushes her fingers, she giggles and yells, "They like me!" I bait one through the lips and toss it to a fishy-looking corner. It dances around for five minutes, nudging the bobber this way and that, and I am sure we are about to nail one. But it never happens. This is evidently bluegill water.

We go looking for worms and hit pay dirt by uprooting sod near a seep downhill from the pond. Emma cannot believe the abundance of the earth. Each new worm sends her into near delirium. "Another one!" she squeals. We put two dozen worms in a cigarette pack we find on the ground.

Three minutes later, the bobber heads south like a share of Enron stock, and we have our first bluegill. "That is a huge fish!" I say of the 5-incher flapping at the end of the line. "A humongous-bungus fish! And you caught it!" All 34 pounds of my daughter are squirming with excitement. I ask if she wants to let it go.

"No! I want to keep it! I want to eat it! Let's catch some more!" We do.

I'm sure there will be other memorable moments in my youngest daughter's life: kindergarten, a first date, graduation, marriage. But I will keep forever the image of Emma's face, of the pure and triumphant delight as she lifted that snapping fish up into the air.

Family life does not linger long upon such summits. That very night, Emma and I tangle over the number of Barbie dolls allowed in the bathtub. I set the bag limit at 10 to delay the inevitable clogging of the drain with synthetic hair. Furious at such tyranny, my daughter screams the worst insult she can think of: "Stupid. Little. DADDY!" Ten minutes later, as I am tucking in the still-damp light of my life, she stirs in her half-sleep and mumbles, "Daddy. Go again tomorrow?"

"Fishing?" I ask.

"Yeah," answers a small voice falling back into slumber. "But first digging worms."

AGING
UNGRACEFULLY

I recently had one of those dangerous ends-in-a-zero birthdays that lure middle-aged guys into taking stock of their lives. This is a dicey business, frequently leading to despair and rash action, such as running off with the babysitter or dropping 60 grand on a candy-apple-red pickup with a Viper V10 engine that will pass anything on the road except a gas station. Me, I went bass fishing, arranging to meet my buddy Greg at a nearby lake.

Greg is a curmudgeon, a painter and sculptor whose work gets high marks from critics but is too candid and straightforward for our sophisticated times. His latest project, for example, is a series of anatomical human hearts about four times life-size, meticulously sculpted in red cedar. A rare hereditary disease in Greg's family caused the hearts to pack it in early, almost before they got started. Eight siblings, including his twin, died in infancy or child-hood. Greg doesn't know how or why he escaped, but he grew up more closely acquainted with death than any kid ought to. His two obsessions, art and fishing, help him cope. Each cedar heart requires thousands of hours of focused solitude with chisels, gouges, and carving burrs. He fishes like he sculpts, so I learned long ago not to promise to be home by a certain hour when I go fishing with him.

The weather on the anniversary of my birth was practically an invitation to self-pity: hot and thermally inverted, a sky the color of plumber's putty holding down air that you didn't want to inhale any more of than necessary. We figured the bass would be deep and set about trying to dredge some up, starting with the closest structure, the riprap where a bridge crosses the lake. Greg was throwing a deep-diving Shad Rap that looked like a perch dressed in drag, and I was slow-rolling a 1/2-ounce spinnerbait. It was too deep to anchor, so we drifted under the bridge, paddled back up, and drifted it again. All the while, Greg ridiculed my spin-nerbait, a lure he considers vulgar. "There is nothing in nature that looks like that. Have you ever in your life caught anything with it?" I told him that I had, as he very well knew but had forgotten because his fragile ego deletes any memory in which he is outfished.

After a spell we headed for a line of standing timber that marked a drowned road and tied up to a dead trunk in 25 feet of water. Greg tied on a Zoom Trick Worm in watermelon gold glitter. For two hours straight we fished without a hit. Finally, at about 7 p.m., the day began to soften. Snapping turtles surfaced and blew bubbles. A bullfrog started honking in the long grass along the bank. Suddenly Greg grunted. "I'm on." A fat 2-1/2-pound bass jumped twice on its way into the boat. Five minutes later something slammed my spinnerbait and started to torpedo this way and that under the surface. It was a tiger muskie about 2 feet long and mad as anything that dinner came with a hook in it. With my spinnerbait mangled, I made a small gesture with my left hand and soon a fresh Zoom slapped me in the back. Such are the advantages of fishing with the same guy for 20 years.

We each set the hook on a few more bass before my cell phone buzzed in my pocket. It was my wife, Jane, who, strangely, asked to speak to Greg. In the stillness of the twilight, I could hear every word. The guests had been waiting at the house for an hour. Had he forgotten?

"Not at all," he said evenly. "Everything's fine." Greg ended the call and handed the phone back. Great. Jane didn't know that relying on Greg to leave off fishing and get me to my own surprise party on time was like asking Michael Jackson to stop hanging out with kids and meet you at a policeman's ball. Even if we paddled back immediately and I broke the speed limit the whole way, I wouldn't be home for another hour. Greg calmly rerigged his worm and tossed it out. "Let's make a few more casts," he said. We did, and by the time I got home, the 30 or so guests still there had switched over to water. The cake was brought out, the song was sung, and they left. Greg, showing a good instinct for self-preservation as well as his usual antisocial tendencies, told me he would see me at the party and went home for the night.

Two days later he called to see if I could meet him on Thursday at the lake. "You know, I think that riprap's beat," he said. "We should just head straight for the wood." I was tempted to point out how he had ruined a good party, nuked a week's worth of planning by my wife, and left a crowd of people cooling their heels — all to chase a green fish. But those decade birthdays will wise you up. What had happened was done, and dredging it up wouldn't change that. You get only so many old friends over a lifetime, and you're lucky to have them. I've been told I'm not always a box of chocolates myself.

WHAT STRANGE CREATURES

The 110th-anniversary issue of America's oldest continuously published hunting and fishing magazine, *Field & Stream,* is already a collector's item. Centuries from now, archaeologists will discover copies carefully preserved in barbershops and beneath the short leg of hunting camp tables across the country. As they study the remains of our culture in these, the final days before our economic collapse and absorption into the Chinese empire as a rural province, what conclusions will they draw about early-21st-century American life? I'm glad you asked.

Our civilization was a mess. Careful excavation (of my house alone) will show that although men of this era possessed the theoretical ability to use sliding-drawer technology, most of us preferred to keep our outdoor gear and everyday clothing strewn randomly over the floor for easy viewing. Bowhunters preferred arrows of as many different length, weight, and fletching configurations as possible, perhaps as a testament to their skills. Guns were thought to shoot better if left uncleaned for years. And any kind of shotgun maintenance was particularly taboo, thought to bring generations of bad luck.

Approximately 75 percent of the U.S. economy depended on revenue generated by hunting gear. Each year, an average sportsman obtained two offroad vehicles, four firearms, three bows, and many times that number of knives and flashlights. These items should have provided years of service but for one surprising characteristic: Sportsmen insisted that they be made in camouflage patterns, so most were lost within hours of the initial purchase, often before the buyer even left the store. Like other great powers, then, the country ultimately collapsed from within. While focused on external threats from men in noncamouflage ski masks, the nation ignored the stupendous cash-sucking power of Realtree Hardwoods HD and Mossy Oak Break-Up at home. Some researchers will theorize that Seclusion Asphalt 4-F, a particularly effective pattern introduced in the culture's last days, might have been secretly developed and imported by our northern rival, the

Molson Brewing Co.

There was a great and universal fear of catastrophic flooding. In all but the most mountainous areas, people maintained finely crafted fiberglass boats on wheeled trailers parked just outside their doors and kept in a constant state of readiness: gas tanks full, tangerine-flake finishes buffed to a high gloss, carbonated beverages iced. Boats were not camouflage, but Americans replaced them annually, even if their houses leaked and they were unemployed. They were stocked with salted emergency rations shaped as worms and lizards, their favorite foods, and outfitted with hatches to store water, which had to be continuously reoxygenated in order for people to metabolize it. The fear of deluge will baffle researchers until they come across fragments of the *Star,* a publication that predicted the future with unerring accuracy. It warned that all the world would be inundated should a temptress named Rosie O'Donnell rise to power.

The wealthiest members of society lived outside urban centers. This rural nobility demonstrated their status by affixing the preserved remains of bass and deer on the walls of their central gathering rooms. Singing electronic largemouths, while rare, were marks of exceptional status. Some excavations will show that when a man married outside his clan, it was the woman who determined whether and where these objects were displayed. In many such cases, the taxidermy was exhibited only in their dwelling's underground recesses.

We believed that whitetail deer and largemouth bass possessed supernatural powers. Shamans placed deer with especially large antlers in the halls adjacent to enormous temples, such as the ones that will be excavated at Springfield, Missouri, and Sidney, Nebraska. Each massive head was displayed along with a number on a brass plaque, such as 195-3/8 or 204-1/8. The significance of these numbers will not be understood, but some archaeologists will hypothesize that the number was the true object of veneration and that the deer merely served as a sort of honor guard.

Heads of American households journeyed to the great antler halls to be taxed several times a year. Men spent much of each year in gymnasiums strengthening their upper bodies in anticipation of these visits. After paying homage to the numbers in the antler hall and gazing at the aisles of miraculous gear, each man was allowed to carry off as much of this treasure as possible in a single load. At the same time, half his annual income was electronically deducted from his bank account. He then underwent a final test of skill, which required him to wander in an outdoor concrete maze for days, looking for his vehicle. Upon finding it, he set down his armload of prizes to unlock and open its vast cargo bay. During the few seconds between putting the merchandise down and turning around to pick it up again, all of the camouflage items would vanish.

ONE MOMENT, PLEASE . . .

No, dear Recorded Lady of the phone company, *you* listen closely because *my* menu options have changed. Press "1" if you think I will be the one to give up first and let you keep charging me for stuff I don't need just because I have been on hold for six hours. I would rather be in my tree stand, but as a hunter I am skilled in the art of waiting. Press "2" if you think I am awash in disposable income and have no need for a new deer rifle. Press "3" if you want to speak to me, a dehydrated but determined hunter who is prepared to wait until the Rapture to fix the automatic leak your company installed in my wallet. Those funds have already been earmarked for the Remington 7600 pump .270 that my friend Ty is selling.

Ah, Recorded Lady, if only we had met under happier circumstances. Instead, I opened my monthly statement from your company (which discretion prevents me from naming, although its initials apparently stand for Making Customers Insane) and discovered that I am paying an extra 99 cents per month for the anachronistic luxury of a paper bill. It was this change that prompted me, many hours ago, to call and switch to online billing. I will continue to hold, because 99 cents a month adds up. Over 25 years, it comes to $297, enough to buy Ty's rifle, with its twin action bars, free-floated barrel, and quick-release four-shot magazine.

Ah, Recorded Lady, you have returned after a short interval of toothless smooth jazz. You explain that my long hold time is due to "an unusually heavy volume of calls." And yet this is the only kind of volume of calls your company experiences. You assure me that, even now, an army of customer-service representatives is engaged in hand-to-hand combat over the privilege of serving me. Meanwhile, exciting news! Did I know that I can register for a chance to win $10,000 just by signing up for DSL service? Actually, Recorded Lady, I do my lottery playing at 7-Eleven, just like everybody else.

Recorded Lady, did you know that the 7600 goes unheralded on virtually all "Greatest Deer Rifles" lists? Yet it is an excellent firearm: inexpensive, accurate, and as dependable as an old rotary phone. What's more, it's a great gun for still-hunting, since it offers faster follow-up shots than any bolt action and even some semiautos. No, Recorded Lady, I do not wish to sign up for the CallManager feature that would allow me to stage miniature United Nations conference calls with nine friends and connect to satellite imaging so I can find lost garden tools in my own backyard. But thanks for asking.

The gun in question is available because of an unfortunate experience Ty had hunting mule deer a few years back in the Montana badlands. Crawling on his belly for half a mile toward a buck with a rack like a Sears dump rake, my friend at last attained the cover of a small rock. He then looked down and saw a rattlesnake occupying the very same real estate. Although the serpent showed no aggressive intent, Ty found himself unable to reciprocate. Emitting one of the louder screams ever made by a surviving licensed electrician, he levitated from prone to standing by force of will alone and clubbed to death what turned out to be a 2-foot hank of barbed wire left over from an old fencing job. The serpent was reduced to rusty powder, the walnut stock sustained extensive rock- and barbed wire-related injuries, and the buck bounced happily out of sight. This experience soured Ty on Montana, mule deer hunting generally, and that 7600 in particular.

Here's the beauty part, Recorded Lady. It still shoots fine, and the very defects that mar its cosmetic appeal make it attractive to tightwads like me. I have always held that the first thing to do with anything new that you love is to go out and bang it against something. Once that initial ding is out of the way, you can get on with enjoying it. (I am sure that unlimited directory assistance in the Islamic Republic of Mauritania, value-priced at $4.99 per month, pays for itself the first time it is used, but I must decline.)

You underestimate me, Recorded Lady. I do not choose to try my call later, when hold times may be reduced. I am a Heavey, of Irish extraction, eldest son of my father, and cheap to the bone. Notice that I do not say "thrifty," Recorded Lady. Thrifty is for dabblers and dilettantes. Among my people, cheapness is not a hobby but a vocation. One of my earliest memories was seeing a look of profound satisfaction spread over the face of my grandfather, a decorated general wounded in both world wars, as he shifted his Oldsmobile into neutral and coasted down hills to save gas. My own father once stopped the car to pick up a fallen apple from the middle of the street. Back home, he doused it with milk, put it in the oven, and served it to my sister and me as "dessert."

These men are my ancestors, Recorded Lady. This is the legacy I strive to be worthy of. And so it is just you and me now, locked in a contest of wills to determine who gets the Remington 7600. Do not think me arrogant, Recorded Lady, but I am betting on me.

Undressed to Kill

No part of *Field & Stream* magazine is more eagerly awaited than the sage advice from the likes of Jerome B. Robinson, Keith McCafferty, and T. Edward Nickens. These are guys who know from personal experience that:

- A bull moose nose is the size of the average human head and, properly tanned, makes a good hat.
- If you happen to survive the crash of your bush plane in Alaska and the pilot does not, it is perfectly acceptable to help yourself to one of his cigars.

I learned some valuable field lessons myself this year that I'd like to pass on. I'm not claiming they rise to the postgraduate level of woodsmanship. But if you're still awaiting a bunk in the gifted-and-talented section of hunting camp, listen up.

Sleep with your clothes on. On a deer hunt in the Adirondacks, Gerald Marcury and I agreed that I would head out before first light, hike to a distant saddle, and ambush any bucks he might push my way while still-hunting. As I sweat easily, I opted to hike in long johns and a wool shirt, then don additional layers as needed. This plan worked perfectly right up until I sat down on a cushion of pine boughs and realized that my Realtree pants were folded atop my Realtree sleeping bag back at camp. Four hours later, Gerald approached, deerless but smiling nonetheless. "Is that a Southern thing, no pants?" he asked.

Six months later, I met up with Gerald and a buddy to have a beer. I started to introduce myself to the friend, who shook my hand warmly and said, "Oh, you're famous. Everybody in the hunt club says, 'You should've seen the guy from *Field & Stream* who forgot his pants.' We even have a saying now." He dropped his voice to a TV-announcer baritone. "Pants: Don't leave home without 'em." (Gerald, allow me to thank you publicly. I have never met a guy who sleeps in women's underwear who is half the hunter you are.)

Hunt with SpongeBob. As I let my daughter Emma off at kindergarten before going hunting one October morning, I pointed up and cried, "Oh, look at the hawk!" Then I palmed the SpongeBob SquarePants Sea Mail Play-a-Sound book she had been reading, which her teachers have forbidden in the classroom. I thought no more about it until I was on stand and realized I had inadvertently stashed the thing in my daypack. After not even seeing a deer all morning, and with nothing to lose, I pushed the button decorated with a giggling Sponge-Bob. Out came a sound like a doe bleat on helium. Intrigued, I hit it again. A doe emerged from the bushes 70 yards distant, where it stood alert and frozen for two minutes. I hit the button once more. Fifteen minutes later, I sent an arrow into that deer. I am unsure about SpongeBob's sexual orientation, but I will say this: The boy knows deer.

Impersonate a competent person. Anybody who hunts with me regularly knows that I am essentially useless. I am physically unimpressive, have the woods sense of a parking meter, and for years thought that a "staging area" was where deer rehearsed theatrical performances. I'm tolerated by other hunters because I know my place and because a natural bent toward arson makes me invaluable in starting and tending campfires. To make up for my defects, I religiously read the tips in *F&S,* then pass them off as my own at every opportunity. Recently, when a friend was lamenting the loss of his scope covers, I plucked an old inner tube from his truck bed, cut out a ring, and wrapped it over the optics, forming a watertight seal (this appeared in the Sportsman's Notebook section of the magazine, October 2005). "Where in the world did you learn that?" he asked, amazed. "Old cowboy trick," I shrugged, affecting the air of a man who had grown up in a sod house on the prairie with Pa riding the range and Ma fighting off Indians.

Shut the bathroom door. Much of my rifle practice occurs with a pellet gun in the basement when nobody else is home. After a session this fall, I was sure my earplugs had migrated almost to my brain. Rushing upstairs to the bathroom mirror, I was probing deep in my auditory canal with a Leatherman Wave when at the door I saw the mother of a child with whom my daughter had evidently missed a play-date. She had entered the house when no one answered. Her face was pretty much the mask of horror you would expect to see upon discovering a man committing suicide via earhole. Her hands were clamped protectively over the eyes of her child, whom she dragged bodily backward through the living room, her mouth moving soundlessly. I watched — but did not hear — the door slam as she fled. I knew it was only a matter of minutes before my wife got word and returned home to deal with the large order of trouble with anchovies and extra cheese I had whipped up. The only question was how to spend the brief interval of peace remaining. I returned to the basement and shot a few more targets. Looking back, it was the smartest thing I did all year.

PATH TO ENLIGHTENMENT

This whole job-marriage-family thing is putting a serious crimp in my deer season. Had I known before what I know now, I might have done things differently. Think of a hunting version of the 1970s TV series *Kung Fu.* Orphaned as a child, I enter a monastery in Iowa, where I learn the secret rites of Unitarian Universalism and purify both mind and body by continuous practice of archery and still-hunting. One day, after besting the emperor's vain eldest son in a 3-D tournament, I am forced to flee, driving first prize: a Dodge SRT-10 Quad Cab (Viper V-10 engine, custom Mossy Oak paint, power-bulge hood, and cigar lighter). I become a nomadic monk, hunting and fishing my way from town to town, teaching the Ten Suggestions that lie at the heart of Unitarianism and encouraging people to form meaningful discussion groups. In time I attract disciples, young men from farming villages who are drawn to my humble dignity and secret knowledge of deer. Eventually, the emperor's son, regretting his rashness, seeks me out to apologize and offer vast sums of —

Jane taps my foot, jolting me back to the fluorescent lights of Parent Participation Night at Emma's kindergarten. My butt, I now notice, has gone numb from the folding metal chair. It no longer belongs to me. It has gone away to become someone else's butt for a time. Like the soul of a shaman, it will return to my body upon completing its quest. Strange that it never goes numb in a tree stand. I could be out there now, 20 feet up and 50 yards inside the timber on a trail leading to what I believe is the last standing patch of corn in the county. Were I not trying to amass credits as a good father (so that I can get back to the woods another time), that's where you would find me. I missed the first day of bow season back in September for a similar meeting, Parent Orientation Night, which was unnecessary in the extreme. Not only did I already know the layout of the school, I had logged it into my Garmin as a waypoint.

Tonight's riveting presentation is something about Preparing Our Children for the Future. Under the new Standards of Learning (official slogan: "Creating a nation of professional test-takers, one worksheet at a time") the school day is now so crammed with opportunities for your child to check the right box that if he or she is tardy more than three times in a semester, you can officially kiss college good-bye and start planning for that career in cosmetology.

I wonder if all this hothouse learning is what my daughter truly needs to flower. Perhaps I should field-school her during October and early November. Liberated from the confines of the classroom, a radio-collared girl running the woods in a zigzag pattern might flush bedded deer my way during the slow midday hours. Mom would not go for it, of course. Nor would some of the more alarmist child-protection people. But they wouldn't necessarily have to know. And Emma, who learns quickly, would probably not need a shock collar after the first couple of outings. She'd be getting healthy exercise, learning about the deer woods, and spending quality time with her dad. A win-win-win situation, and only during archery season, of course, because Emma's welfare comes first.

The meeting finally ends. The spirit of my butt returns to its corporeal home. At the school playroom, a quietly fuming sub hands us our little monster, whose legs are encrusted with paste, glitter, and paint. "Like the circus girl," Emma chirps.

We get home and see that our neighbor has put up an electric Christmas reindeer, a motorized wire skeleton covered with tiny white lights that turns its head every 15 seconds. As Jane precedes us into the darkened house, I grab my daughter's shoulder.

"Emma," I whisper, hunkering down next to her. "Deer! Don't move. Let's sneak on it." There is a lone pine sapling between us and our quarry. Using it to shield our movements and waiting until the deer looks away, we begin the stalk. Emma totally gets it, staying low, using a slow heel-to-toe weight transfer, and freezing when the deer looks back. Once we've gained the tree, I tell her that it's too open for us to stalk together. She must go on alone. If she can touch its flank undetected, count coup like the Indians, she will have passed a great test as a hunter. She nods solemnly and steps out at the deer's next movement. Two turns later, she touches the glowing haunch. "Did it!" she crows.

"Whoo-hoo!" I shout. "Emma! Hunter! Circus girl! Deer stalker!" I swing her up in my arms and back to the house. As I take her inside, she asks, "C'we go hunting again tomorrow?"

"Sure, monkey," I answer, suddenly overcome by love for this child who has descended from the heavens to ruin my deer season, to complicate and enrich my life beyond all measure. "You and me, we're going to sneak on every deer in the neighborhood."

■ ■ ■ ■

V
MAKING
INCOMPETENCE PAY:
THE WELL-SEASONED
SPORTSMAN

■ ■ ■ ■

THE FAT MAN

Any time you throw together a bunch of guys who don't know one another in hunting camp, it takes a bit of scratching and sniffing before the top dog emerges. I have been in this situation often enough to know three things about the process:

1. I am not in the running.
2. The initial front-runner rarely holds the lead for long.
3. Watch out for the fat guy.

I was recently hunting caribou above the Arctic Circle in Alaska (a phrase, incidentally, that I now work into every conversation I have, including with whomever is on the other end of the intercom at the big red drive-up menu at Wendy's) when I found myself sharing a tent with Steve Freese, 56, a newly retired Douglas County, Nebraska, cop, who clocks in at 5-foot-8 and about

245. He has the widest-set eyes I've ever seen on a human and a head like a bowling ball.

The younger men figured that putting the two hunters most at risk for rapid-onset Alzheimer's in the same tent was a no-brainer, which suited us fine. Young guys invariably assume their lives are unique and fascinating, but older guys know that, superficial differences aside, we're really all as alike as eggs.

The superficial difference between Steve and me was that I spent 10 minutes each morning rooting around in my duffel for any socks and underwear that might have been miraculously freshened by 24 hours in a tightly packed bag, while Steve would simply fillet a vacuum-sealed plastic pouch and remove clean socks and long johns. He had made these packets up using a Cabela's food vacuum sealer. "Handiest damn thing you ever saw," he said. "Food is just the beginning."

As we all sat around the fire the first night, Steve sipped a Beam-and-Sam's-Club-cola. One of his last duties as a police captain, he said, had been as a trainer, whipping new recruits into shape before they could hurt themselves or, more important, older cops. "First thing, I'd ask them, 'How many of you guys have heard that there's no such thing as a stupid question?' And they'd be so eager, you know, just clawing over each other to get their hands up first. 'Well, that's a bunch of bull crap,' I'd tell them. 'Your best move for the next two years is to shut up and listen.' "

Later, we all weighed in with our hunting plans and ambitions. Steve opined that he was as likely to take a caribou close to camp as not; other factors being equal, he preferred less hauling to more. Sure enough, at about 2 p.m. the next day, he dropped a heavily racked bull just 350 yards from camp. Hearing the shot, I hustled over to help, arriving in about 20 minutes. By that time, Steve was cleaning his fingernails with his knife. At his feet lay four neatly butchered quarters, hide still on to protect the meat, and a small mountain of expertly cut tenderloins, backstraps, neck roasts, and rib meat. Nearby were the clean, white bones of his bull, innards intact. It was astounding knife work. "You didn't gut him," I said, making my daily entry in the Stating the Obvious Sweepstakes.

"Just more work," he replied.

I made him a deal on the spot that I'd carry his meat if he'd help butcher mine. When they saw the carcass, most of the other guys followed suit. The fat man's stock had begun to rise. Steve also turned out to be the best cook in camp, pushing it higher still. It was as if he had known all along he would be the lead dog and couldn't be bothered to compete. Pretty soon, he had only to casually note that we were running low on water or that a pan needed cleaning before one of us, me included, would quietly hop to. One of the younger guys, handing him a Beam-and-Sam's-Club after Steve had made the venison fall off the guy's bull like it was overcooked stew meat, asked if the drink was mixed to his liking. Steve nodded deeply, then threw me a little wink as if to say, *Rookies. You gotta love them.*

Everybody ended up taking a bull, some as far as 2 miles away over the tundra. None was as big as Steve's. Last I heard, at least two of the guys had bought vacuum sealers, along with a large supply of gallon bags. Steve says those are the perfect size for a change of socks and long johns.

I called Steve recently and got him in a duck blind along the Missouri River, where he was hunting, evidently in the company of a cop he had once ridden with. "Hang on a sec, Bill," he said. Gusts of wind buffeted the mouthpiece, then I heard that familiar voice calling: "Same rules as in the squad car, Kevin. If the weather turns bad and we've only got one raincoat, it's mine." It sounded as if the fat man was doing just fine.

A MISSED
CONNECTION

Not long ago, the editor in chief of *Field & Stream,* Sid Evans, invited me on a two-and-a-half-day deer hunt at his father's club in Mississippi. To understand what an editor is like, picture an Afghan warlord — bloodthirsty, cunning, perpetually bent on revenge — plying his dark art in a room decorated with the trophy skulls of his enemies. Lose the turban, give him some skin-care products and a little dental work, and — *voila!* — say hello to the boss. But make no mistake. The dynamics are unchanged. When he issues an invitation to me, a humble foot soldier, I accept instantly.

The plan was to meet up at the Memphis airport with Evans's father, John, drive south to the 6,000-acre club near the Mississippi River that he shares with about 30 other members, and hunt the muzzleloader season. I met Sid and both of his parents at baggage claim, and we caravanned to a barbecue joint for massive quantities of pulled pork and coleslaw. For an editor, Sid comes from amazingly upright stock. His father, affable and easygoing, is a diehard bow-hunter and fisherman. His mother is a woman of goodwill, beauty, and charm. I doubt that these were his real parents.

After lunch, the men loaded up and drove south into Coahoma County. As we crossed the great hump of a levee, I resolved to ingratiate myself with the actor portraying John Evans because that guy has a gate key to 10 square miles of deer heaven — bottomland hardwoods under intense QDM. Members shoot only bucks 4-1/2 years old or older.

Sid and I shared a room at camp. "Fair warning, I snore like a bear," I said. (I was looking forward to tormenting his sleep, as he so frequently ruins mine with 4 p.m. e-mails suggesting a quick total rewrite of a story by the next morning.) "Me, too," he answered brightly. Then he rolled over and fell instantly asleep, an ability common to Stalin, Hitler, and other despots. Disturbingly rhythmic snoring kept me awake for hours.

Dark and early the next morning, we headed out to stands where good bucks had been seen recently. "You snore like a damn chain saw," I told Sid.

"Really? You were moaning all night," he answered. "Sounded like a crazy woman having a bad night at bingo." This was all the more embarrassing because it was probably true, as my wife has reported similar sounds.

I had brought my bow along, a not-so-subtle reminder that I possess a skill Sid has yet to master. After a full day afield during which nobody saw a buck, I decided that the point had been made and asked his "dad" if I could borrow an extra muzzleloader. I had revenge in mind. On our only other outing together, Sid had boated a big tarpon, while I had demonstrated why I should never be given a loaded fly rod. But the rut was winding down, and the second day passed with little more activity than the first.

On the final morning we just had time for a three-hour hunt before dashing back to Memphis. I sat in a ladder stand overlooking a promising brushy area. With 15 minutes left, a set of big brown antlers popped into sight, headed toward me through the tangle. My view was lateral, offering no indication of width. Nor, in those few moments, could I count tines. But the prison break in my chest said that this was a shooter. The buck came quickly up out of a small gully and stood for a moment in an opening 80 yards off. As the crosshairs settled on his chest, I fired. He galloped off and was gone. From sighting to shot had taken all of about eight seconds. Sid came over at the sound, and together we madly searched the area for sign until we were in real danger of missing our flights. All we found were a few clipped hairs where the buck had stood.

To his credit, Sid seemed genuinely sympathetic. "You've been shooting a bow all year instead of a rifle. And you'd never even shot this gun before. It happens." I began wondering if the boss possibly was a mammal after all. Speeding to the airport, we slapped together sandwiches from a cooler in the back, and I slipped the man playing his father my business card, just in case. Once past security, Sid and I shook hands and headed for our gates. After about 30 feet, something made me turn and look back. Sid had stopped too. He smiled slightly and, as if at last freed from the role of gracious host, suddenly grabbed his throat and stuck out his tongue — the universal "You Choked" taunt. Then he was gone.

I was completely flummoxed. Not by the

insult itself, a thing of no particular conse-
quence. What unnerved me was that it was
exactly the kind of thing I would have done.

POOR RICHARD

Last summer, Jack Unruh, illustrator of my monthly magazine column, and I, with no more sense than a couple of babies playing with steak knives, convinced ourselves to take a pheasant hunting road trip to North Dakota in October. We talked it up over the phone until we fell for our own B.S. about pheasants that had never seen a hunter and dogs leaping through the prairie grass. Then, the week before the trip, we both came clean. I admitted I had never actually hunted pheasants. Jack mentioned that his dogs were "unfinished."

"Willy Mae points when she's in the mood but won't hold it. Rudy is like her, only without as good a nose. Plus he pees on my leg sometimes. It's a dominance thing." He had also realized that he had better pack a sandwich, as the 1,300-mile drive from Dallas to Bismarck might take an entire afternoon.

To break up the trip, Jack invited his friend Richard Stucky along. Richard is an independent farmer in Pretty Prairie, Kansas, population 604. He doesn't make much money or get off the farm often, and we sort of patted ourselves on the backs for including him, as if we had started a Take a Farmer Hunting Foundation.

Actually, Richard — a stocky, slow-talking fellow about my age who looks younger, probably because he isn't worried all the time — hardly detracted from the trip at all. His 100-pound German shorthair mix, Dusty, was a dream dog. "Who trained that critter?" I asked Richard one day, as Dusty released a rooster into his hand. "Me," he said. Turns out that Dusty gets almost daily practice in season on the quail that Richard raises and hunts on the farm. Depending on what he and his wife, Connie, feel like eating, he also goes after deer, ducks, geese, and rabbits. He has a bass boat and four coonhounds. I was losing sympathy for poor Richard by the minute. Jack volunteered that his friend was the only guy he'd ever known who'd worn out a shotgun. "And he did it on birds alone. No targets."

I asked Richard about farming. "There's no money in it, but I'd die if I had to get a desk job. I've got about 200 acres of my own and lease another thousand. Wheat. And I do custom harvesting to subsidize the farming. But it pretty much lets me hunt whenever I want to."

"So you have all those big machines?"

"Yeah."

"Aren't you sort of screwed if one breaks down?"

"Well, you just have to fix it."

It turns out that poor old Richard could fix just about anything: green hunting dog, combine, or clogged motel ice machine. He permanently fixed any pheasant that got up within 40 yards of his battered, no-name side-by-side. "Secondhand. Fella at the gun shop said it's a Belgian. Little shorter stock and a lower comb. Fits me good, especially in heavy clothes."

We soon discovered that he was also the best judge of public-land cover likely to hold birds, so Richard rode shotgun, Jack drove, and I slept in the back. Richard got his three-bird limit every day, often before lunch. Jack limited out some days. And several times I scared a bird so severely with my first two shots that it committed suicide by flying back into the third. Richard, seeing how spastic I became every time a feathered Improvised Explosive Device went off at my feet, had to bite his lip to keep from laughing. "You gotta relax, Bill," he finally said. "They hardly ever attack people."

One afternoon, I asked Richard about the shotgun Jack had mentioned. "Dad bought me that gun new, a Franchi, back in 1967 when I was 12. And eventually the little hook in the receiver block that pulls the empty shell just broke off. I got a 1D 4-inch chunk of key stock, cut it, and filed it down to about the size and shape I needed. And then I got a torch and tempered it, guessing how hard it —"

"Wait," I said. *"You tempered it?"*

"Sure. That's where you —"

"I know what tempering is, Richard." I sat there both admiring and resenting this damn hayseed of a man, a guy who hardly ever left Kansas but knew things I would never know, who was overflowing with kindness and wisdom and vitality. I suddenly felt like a 50-year-old puppy, a bird dog not yet broken from a bad habit of chasing the wrong animals: fame, money, and stuff. I didn't know how to explain this feeling and knew better than to try.

"Listen, Richard. Did I ever tell you about the home theater system I carved out of a pumpkin? Nine speakers, 400 watts, great big flat plasma screen . . ."

Richard just chuckled and shook his head, amused by how some people get themselves all worked up over the simplest things. "You're a hoot, Bill. I swear. You really are." Five minutes later, he told Jack to pull over. "Oughta be some birds in this one," he said. He opened the box and Dusty hit the ground running.

Why Knot?

Like many ineffectual people, I am addicted to the transitory endorphin buzz that comes from impressing somebody besides my own mother. Such moments live in my memory for decades — mostly because they are so few in number. Here's one. Driving back from a canoe trip 30 years ago, our party suddenly noticed tackle boxes, pots, and stuff sacks bouncing off the blacktop behind us, courtesy of a burst zipper in our canvas cartop carrier. While the braver souls dodged traffic to retrieve gear, I scrounged pieces of rope from the trunk, joined them with sheet bends, and tied a bowline loop in one end. Cramming everything back into the carrier, I tossed the line over and around the rack and cinched the whole thing down with a taut-line hitch, the knot you use on tent pegs. It was not the best knot for the application, but it was all I knew. More important, it got us home. And for a few memorable minutes, I reveled in the quiet awe of my companions. I suspect this is how the inventor of the glazed doughnut felt.

In today's world of duct tape, quick-release belts, and bungee cords, no skill demonstrates manly competence so quietly but conclusively as the ability to make rope do your bidding. Knowing this, I recently began buying books on the subject: *The Klutz Book of Knots, The Morrow Guide to Knots,* and others. Eventually, I discovered *The Ashley Book of Knots:* 640 pages, 3,854 knots, and 7,000 illustrations. Published in 1944, it has reigned unchallenged ever since. It is the bible, encyclopedia, and mother of all knot books.

It's also the kind of tome that any guy with mild obsessive-compulsive tendencies (i.e., any fisherman or hunter) might take into the bathroom, along with a piece of rope, fully intending to be back on task momentarily. Days later, he could emerge to discover that his wife had taken the kids to her mother's, the phone had been cut off, and two guys from the electric company were pounding on the door. Such is the hold that knot knowledge can exert.

I began honing my skills immediately on the subjects at hand: my daughter and my dog. Emma, only 6, was so hypnotized by the televised adventures of SpongeBob that it scarcely registered as I loosely wrapped a constrictor knot around her ankle. This simple arrangement exerts a ratchet-like grip when tightened on any curved surface. And tighten it is exactly what Emma suddenly did, returning to her physical body and flailing with great energy. The knot performed as advertised, my daughter went bonkers, and it was only by immobilizing her in a scissors grip with my own legs that I kept her still long enough to undo the aptly named knot. In return for a dinner consisting solely of raspberry Fruit Roll-Ups and Fudgsicle pops, however, she agreed not to inform Mommy.

Thereafter, I confined my efforts to the dog. I secured Snoop's initial compliance with the hobble knot (No. 226), long used by cowboys. My ultimate goal was the double diamond hitch (No. 416), the gold standard among packers for lashing side packs and a riding load, such as a barrel, to a mule. Not wishing to overload the dog, now 12, I substituted sofa pillows for packs and a 72-ounce Quaker Oatmeal cylinder (available at any Costco) for the barrel. Again, unforeseen difficulties arose. After the sixth crossing, I had to consult the book for the next step. Snoop, who is at an age when she no longer suffers fools, sensed her opportunity and administered a small but authoritative bite to my hand before hobbling off to her lair under the sideboard.

I next attempted No. 442, by which a game animal is lashed to a tote pole with clove hitches, useful to know in country too rough for dragging. The perfect stuffed animal in Emma's inventory for this purpose was a lavender unicorn about the size of a yearling doe. The arrangement was a success, but even I had to admit a unicorn looks sad bound and hanging upside down from an old broomstick. I felt as if I'd trussed up innocence itself and freed the mythical beast without showing my handiwork to anyone.

I was in despair over my prospects of ever impressing anyone again when a strange thing happened. One night, over at my parents' house, Emma and I went into their garage for a pump to inflate her new Bounce-oline, an injury-inducing toy my sister had bought. Noticing that the garage door had been left open yet again, I pulled the rope and shut it. Emma had never even been in a garage before. To see an entire wall of a room suddenly appear, slide shut, and slam into place was, to her, a revelation. "Whoa!" she cried. "What knot was that?"

I paused, but only for a moment. "A very special one," I said as endorphins began bathing my brain in a sense of well-being. "That is the ancient and powerful daddy knot."

THE ENFORCER

An Internet dating service would never have paired us. There's me: married with kids, heavily mortgaged, and semi-gainfully employed. There's Paula: none of the above. Gruff, gravel-voiced, somewhere in her mid-50s, Paula Smith dresses like a river rat and has all the charm of a sawmill foreman. But come spring, I'd gladly take a date with her over Angelina Jolie, because Paula is the best shed hunter I've ever met.

She is a woman of mystery and some danger. I first met her about 10 years ago, when she washed up at Fletcher's Boat House like an unmoored canoe on the spring floods, and the regulars, smelling the woods sense on her, took her in. She fishes the river and tramps the woods in season for berries, mushrooms, nuts, and greens. On busy weekends at the boathouse, they press her into working the dock. Even the rowdiest anglers know better than to mess with Paula. But her real job is custodian and protector of the local bucks from poachers working the woods. She keeps year-round tabs on both. And if she has to sneak past warning signs or under fences, if she has to get threatened or yelled at, so be it. The only place she will not go is the CIA campus across the river in Langley. "Don't even think about it, honey," she once told me. "Trust me."

Sometimes she wrecks poachers' blinds. Sometimes she just places telltale vines on their paths to pattern them before she acts. Last year she found a stashed bow and turned it in. The year before, she told a warden friend how best to stake out another illegal hunter. They arrested that guy. Deer hunting, she says, is nothing compared to hunting poachers.

She stubs out a cigarette as I drive up to where she is boarding, slides in, and shows me photos of her latest finds. There are matched sets of the trophy sheds she routinely collects, plus an unusual number of roadkills this year. One is a honker 12-point ("21 with stickers") with a yardstick in his rack to verify the spread: 24 inches. "Found him a few yards off a yuppie trail in Rock Creek Park," she says. In Paula's world, yuppies are just another species in the urban forest, like raccoons or possums, only less alert.

We drive into Rock Creek Park. In the woods behind a park police substation she quickly locates a big 4-point shed. It's fresh, traces of cartilage still rimming the pedicel. But she is unhappy with the area. "We should be finding more. Somebody beat us to it." We relocate a mile away. She crawls through a hole in a fence into woods belonging to some huge mansion or embassy. "Look big," she whispers. "There's a monster here if somebody didn't kill him." She finds two chewed little sheds, last year's. I find the dried-up carcasses of a doe and a raccoon, and one dead Samsung cell phone. Then Paula holds up half a carbon shaft with a rusty broadhead. "Shot from the ridge across the road," she whispers. "Even the poachers don't come in here." We keep looking, eventually exiting via another hole in the fence. She shakes her head. "An 11-pointer was living in there. We should have found his sheds." We finish by working our way down into thicker cover, briers and honeysuckle by the creek. She whistles me over to see a blind. I don't buy it at first.

"I'm telling you, honey. Smart poachers never cut stuff, they rearrange what's already there. And branches don't fall like this." I'm thinking maybe Paula has had her oatmeal in the microwave too long, that she has poachers on the brain. Then I see the salt block sitting in a shooting lane at 15 yards. I am — to put it mildly — blown away. For a guy in my life situation, I spend a scandalous amount of time in the woods. Comparatively, however, I'm a greenhorn. Crazy, cranky Paula is playing the deer game at the grand-master level.

Meanwhile, pulled by some intuition, she has disappeared. I locate her 90 yards upstream, kneeling over a small mound of brown fur and white bone. "Bastard just took the head," she says, poking the remains with a stick. She stirs the pile and reveals a crossbow bolt. "They usually don't leave the arrow. Might have gotten spooked." The good news is that the hooves are too small for it to have been the 11-pointer. The bad is that the poacher might have gotten him, too. She'll give the arrow to her warden friend. The salt block goes in the trunk.

She is silent on the way back. I'm still trying to wrap my head around the fact that she's right, that an invisible army of poachers is beheading deer 10 yards from major roads.

"Sorry we didn't find more," she says, getting out and handing me the 4-point antler as a present. "But there's one good thing. I know who I'll be hunting this fall."

DEATH AND FISHING

Did you ever have one of those days on the water when you happened to be in exactly the right place at exactly the right time and caught fish until you were sick of it? Me neither. I used to think I'd do pretty much anything to get a day like that. But when the chance came this season, I passed it up. Twice, actually. Once was an act of simple economic self-preservation. The other, darker and more mysterious, involved death, a lawn mower, and the unspoken obligations a man takes on if he wants to look himself in the eye while shaving.

The first time, friends who are seriously dialed in to the annual run of white perch up the Potomac invited me out. There are a couple of days a year when — tide, sun, wind, and thermometer aligning — the river may turn into a "silver tide," with schools of perch so thick that the water changes color.

"Tomorrow could be the day," Paula said.

"Meet me and Gordon at the boathouse dock at 10 a.m." As a freelancer, I am absolute sovereign and master of my time. Until I am late filing a story, that is, at which point I turn into Chicken Little, sure that the evening sun will find me standing by the highway with the tools of my new profession: a squeegee, a plastic cup, and a cardboard sign reading, GOD BLESS AND HAVE A NICE DAY. Such being the case at that moment, I said I'd try to be down by 1 o'clock.

When I finally got there, I was told my friends had just left with a cooler full of fish. The tide was slackening, not a good sign for the perch fishing. But I was there, so I rented a boat, rowed into the current, and dropped anchor. I tied on a tandem rig of brown bucktail jigs with a 1-ounce weight, and something hit the moment the sinker touched bottom. Thirty seconds later, I had a jumbo flapping in the bottom of the boat. It was nearly a foot long, a meal in itself. I bumped its head on the gunnel and cast again. Ten minutes later, another. My hands were shaking. I couldn't believe this was happening. In an hour, six very big perch were splayed around my feet. It wasn't the silver tide, but it was the best perch fishing I'd ever had.

Then it stopped. I lost a few jigs in the rocks without even getting a bump and got back just in time to meet my daughter Emma as she stepped off the school bus. Filleted, lightly breaded, and fried, the perch made a splendid dinner.

It rained for two days straight thereafter, ruining the fishing and darkening my mood. Then word came that the mother of our next-door neighbor Dave had died suddenly. A routine checkup a month earlier had turned up a rare heart ailment. She passed away almost before she understood what was going on. After the funeral, Dave stayed on at her house for a few days to make some arrangements as her executor.

Meanwhile, the river had cleared, and it looked like I would get one last shot at the silver tide. Paula called. "Get your butt down here if you still want some perch. They won't be in for long." No longer on deadline, I headed for the car. Then I saw my neighbor's lawn, which had grown tall and lush almost overnight from the rain.

Like most people in the suburbs, Jane and I aren't really tight with our neighbors. We chat across the fence about our kids, but I don't think either family has had the other over for a meal in the 10 years we've lived here. But I remember a day nearly eight years ago, returning home from the funeral for Lily, our daughter who died of SIDS one day shy of her fourth month. When we pulled into the driveway, Dave was there, his face wet and contorted in grief. He walked over and gave me a fierce, wordless hug. That had meant more to me than all the flowers and cards and casseroles we received in those awful days.

Now it was Dave's turn to absorb the hammer blow of sudden death. And the first thing he would see when he pulled into his driveway tomorrow was an overgrown yard. I took my gear back inside, fired up the mower, and cut his lawn. It didn't take much time, just enough to miss out on the fishing. Dave had probably forgotten that long-ago moment, but it will stay with me forever. I was grateful to be able to repay the debt. As I finished, his wife, Beth, drove up with the kids. "You didn't have to do that, Bill," she scolded.

"Actually," I said, "I did."

Invent This

Every year, *Field & Stream* publishes its gear issue, when the otherwise-unemployable "experts" at the magazine review and recommend stuff so silly you'd think we'd all be doing major time at Club Fed for waste, fraud, and abuse. Strangely, that doesn't happen. What happens instead is that semi-nomadic hunter-anglers in barbershops and outhouses come across what we have written and — far more often than you would believe possible — go buy the stuff. Meanwhile, somewhere on a beach in the South of France, the guys who thought up and marketed this junk receive the latest sales numbers and laugh so hard they wet their thongs. (Like I said, it's France.)

This got me thinking: Why doesn't somebody come up with new gear that would actually enhance the outdoor experience for us regular guys? A few modest proposals:

Do-it-all broadhead. It can take hundreds

of hours on stand before you send an arrow into a deer. When you finally succeed, your reward shouldn't be more work. That's why you need a broadhead that not only kills cleanly but also guts, dresses, butchers, and wraps your deer meat. Wouldn't it be nice to arrive at the end of a blood trail to find a perfectly caped buck and a stack of wrapped, labeled venison ready for the freezer? The new arrowhead would come in steak-cut or roast-cut models. Possible name: the Butcherator.

Exploding-scent Frisbee. Look, they already make silly string in an aerosol can that smells like buck or doe urine. That's fine as far as it goes (and a superb addition to any long car trip involving children). But a guy in a tree stand needs more reach than what you get from a can. We need flying disks made of a scent-releasing polymer that shatters explosively upon impact. You'd get the ability to deliver scent-bomb payloads up to 100 yards away without spreading your own scent and, because of the banking flight characteristics of the disk itself, the ability to navigate around thickets, large trees, etc. Possible name: Urine Orbit.

Automated lure rescuer. The average angler loses about $600 worth of lures annually to the kleptomaniacal woody plants known as "trees." Ideally, Congress would pass a law imposing a $1,000 fine on any shrub, domestic or imported, found in possession of a fishing hook. For now, at least, lure-snagging timber is getting a free ride. That's why we need Lure Un-Snagging Technology (L.U.S.T.) robots on every bass boat. A consortium of scientists at the University of Pennsylvania has actually developed a small, tree-climbing robot. And the boys in white coats obviously looked to nature when designing the thing because it has six little motorized legs and a tail that helps it balance. If each of us buys one, the economy of scale could drive the price below $5,000 in no time at all. Possible name: the L.U.S.T. Possum.

The stand-in. Any guy — married or single — knows a successful relationship with a woman of the opposite sex requires an ungodly amount of face time. I personally have several friends who required hospitalization for stress exhaustion after exceeding their intimacy threshold. (One, sadly, was never the same again. He went back to school, became a psychologist, and joined a local theater group that has been performing *Cats* twice a week for eight years.) This is all the more tragic in light of new research showing that females primarily require the mere physical presence of their partner, punctuated by occasional oral and physical cues that indicate he is paying attention.

Enter the remote-controlled, adjustable, full-body spouse decoy. The stand-in ships to your door dressed in jeans and an untucked flannel shirt. Cranial hair can be adjusted for length and male-pattern baldness, and comes with an easy-to-use dye kit. The face features a three-day stubble. Up to 50 pounds of attachable stomach padding allow the substitute to be customized to resemble users with waist sizes from 28 to 56 inches. Its lifelike rubber hands are molded to grip a TV clicker that automatically channel surfs every 15 minutes. Motors in the face randomly portray a range of emotions: approval, interest, surprise, and concern. When activated by the sound of female speech, the digitized voice emits phrases such as: "That sounds like a great idea, babe!" "Tell me more about that, honey." "Imagine that!" "So how did that make you feel?" Programmable for up to two weeks. Comes in married and single versions. Possible names: Dream Daddy and Better Boyfriend.

I have more ideas but can't share them just now. The sales figures should be here soon and I need to go thong shopping.

The Bonehead

Saying "bonefishing in the Bahamas" to the average fly-fisherman is a little like saying "naked touch football with Jessica Simpson" to the average adolescent male. The eyes glaze over, the face assumes a dreamy expression, and drool may begin to form. Having just returned from three days of this exact experience (fishing, not the other one), I can report that it was indeed memorable. And should you currently lack the five grand or so the trip requires, fear not. You can get a surprisingly accurate feel for this kind of angling right at home.

- Go to the brightest, hottest place you can find (a shopping-mall parking lot in Phoenix on an August afternoon works well). Wearing long sleeves and pants, stand crouched and motionless, holding an 8-weight fly rod at the ready. Note how the sweat from your brow washes a refreshing stream of sunblock into the eyes.

- Every hour or so, select an arbitrary spot the size of a butter plate 70 feet upwind and allow yourself one false cast to hit it with a pink No. 6 Crazy Charlie.
- When your cast fails to land smack on target, bang your head slowly and repeatedly against the nearest light pole. This is how you feel when your guide clucks his tongue in disappointment and says, "Nice try." (Which is Bahamian for "God, please don't tell me I have to spend all day with this guy.")
- Repeat for 8 hours daily until deranged.

It goes without saying that I did not pay my own way on this trip. Along with a number of fly-fishing writers and editors, I was a guest of the Orvis Co. I mention this freely to demonstrate my integrity. On the other hand, Orvis does make the finest fishing tackle on earth, as well as superlative gift baskets ("Give the pesto lover in your life the ultimate collection!"); fine dog apparel, such as the World War II Mechanic's Sweater with Zambezi Twill patches at the elbows; and a full line of window treatments.

On the first day of fishing it was immediately clear that there were two skill levels in our group: (1) everybody else and (2) me. Upon receiving complementary 8-weight Zero Gravity fly rods and Vortex VO2 reels, the others were quickly casting all 105 feet of fly line as easily as tying their shoes. Rather than humiliate myself in public, I took the stuff to my room, stared at it, and began calculating its value on eBay if it remained unopened. As this was not an option, I assembled the four-piece rod and accidentally stuck the tip into the ceiling fan. Remarkably, it didn't break, but the noise attracted my hosts. I explained that nothing so rigorously tests a rod as short roll casts in a room with 8-foot ceilings.

Then it was time to go fishing. Fly-fisher folk love bones for the following reasons: You pursue them in places that cost a fortune to access; they are considered inedible; and they spook quicker than Iraqi traffic cops. Casts must be perfect. A foot too long and the fish won't see it. A foot too short and the fish hauls fins for deeper water. Get it just right and . . . well, I have no idea what happens then. Anyway, you stand on the bow of a boat while your guide poles you along mangrove flats shimmering in the tropical heat, spots the fish, and then politely abuses you for failing to instantly cast where he indicated.

The guide I remember best was named Glister, with whom I fished on a particularly infernal day. Glister was very laid back until he saw a bonefish, whereupon he started barking orders like Donald Trump on meth: "Long cast, 9 o'clock. Now!" It took me three false casts to get any line out at all, by which time the fish was gone. "Pah!" he spat, shaking his head. An hour later, given another opportunity, I rushed my back cast and the line balled up at my feet. "Whisha!" Glister grunted. (*Whisha?* I thought. *Is that some voodoo word? Or the first part of "Whisha hadn't gotten stuck with you"?*) I dared not meet his gaze but continued to crouch at the ready.

After another two hours, Glister spotted more fish, a pod of them. "Buncha big fish, 11 o'clock. Twenty yards. No, not eight! Eleven! Again! Let it lie . . . now strip, strip, strip! Stop! Cast again! Farther left. No! Left, left! Shoot that line! Shoot it! Long strip! Stop! Let it lie! Short strips! Strip, strip, strip!" The fish, seeing my line, went screaming away over the flats. "Pah!" spat Glister.

Then he said something I will never forget. "You got to *relax,* man!"

Disoriented from the heat, miserable, nearly blind from the sunblock in my eyes, I tried to respond. But my tongue had joined my fly casting in a land beyond my jurisdiction. The words that eventually came from my mouth were "I . . . spinfishing man . . . most time."

To which Glister observed, "Whisha!"

DOG YEARS

My father's mind is slipping away, cell by cell, and as the architecture fragments and falls he often speaks of dogs. "George didn't come home last night," he says when I come over for Sunday dinner. His hands, which once guided jet fighters to night landings on aircraft carriers, fumble distractedly at the drawstring of his pajama pants. I kiss him and sit at the foot of the bed he can no longer leave unaided. "We went for a walk last night and he got after a raccoon or something. Jerked the leash right out of my hand. And you know how he chases cars." He lies back against the pillows, staring anxiously at the faint cracks in the ceiling plaster, as if he might find an answer there if only he could remember the question.

"It's okay, Dad," I lie. "George was at the front door when I showed up. He's asleep in the basement right now." George, the first dog our family had, died 35 years ago.

"Well, that's good," he says. "We've got to take better care of that dog."

This, I've learned, is how the mind unravels. Events from long ago move into the foreground, while the present seems to vanish even as it unrolls. My father is 86, the last in a line of five generations of career military men. None hunted or fished seriously, but they all loved dogs. On my father's dresser there is a photo of the beloved terrier he had as a boy. "Old Pat," I remember him saying when I was growing up. "What a dog." Early on I came to regard dogs as almost holy creatures: innocent, guileless, incorruptible. They earned their keep simply by existing. You walk into the kitchen and a tail thumps the linoleum with unconditional love. To Dad, this was a stronger case for redemption than any ever made from a pulpit.

George, the first in a long series, was an unruly, stout-hearted brown mutt of middling size who must have had some border collie mutant gene, for he lived to chase cars, and he liked to work close. He would sprint along, inches from a front hubcap, then turn his head in front of the tire, barking as if trying to turn the lead sheep in a flock. My sister and I lived in terror that he would die that way. He did get hit once, limping home after two days and scratching feebly at the back door. But he made it to 15 and died in his sleep.

Suddenly I'm remembering, too. I'm 9, and Dad and I are out fishing in a canoe on Lake Champlain when George chews through the screen door of the summer rental cottage. Panicked at being left behind, he leaps off a 6-foot cliff, paddles out to us, and nearly capsizes the boat as we hoist him aboard. Reunited with his masters, he smiles and shakes, drenching us. Then seven years later, my father and I are digging a hole out back under the forsythia bushes where George liked to lie in wait for cars and mailmen. I already know it is useless to try to stop the tears as I stand on the spade with both feet to slice through the roots.

And so came an endless parade of brown and black pound dogs. There was Fred, the goofy basset who became sexually aroused by the presence of unfamiliar guests in the living room and would sometimes try to mount them. His short legs were deceptive. Fred was a big galoot and impressively endowed. A proper Southern lady, my mother had been taught to simply ignore crude behavior, and guests were left to follow suit according to their abilities.

There was Tilley, who lifted an entire

boneless turkey roast off the counter when my mother turned her back to answer the phone and was out the back door by the time Mom turned back. Dad had to take us to a restaurant that night. Emma, a black mutt, heartbreakingly sweet and soulful with 2-inch eyelashes, had a habit of leaning into you to maximize contact as you watched TV together. Hank, the latest, is a gruff longhaired terrier mix whom we believe was abandoned and lived wild for a time. He snarls and bites reflexively if startled while sleeping and shakes uncontrollably during thunderstorms. Otherwise, like all dogs, he is pure of heart. A surprise birthday present to Dad on his 75th, Hank lived with me for several days before the presentation. We bonded, and now he whines with delight when he sees me, then sounds his loud, hacking bark and turns circles until he calms down.

My father's world has shrunk to the rooms he has lived in for 40 years but no longer recognizes, the immediate family and two vaguely familiar caregivers, and the dogs living and dead who still walk by his side. After dinner, I help Sam, the wonderful Ghanaian man who watches Dad at night, put him back in bed. As I leave, I kiss my father good night and tell him I love him, two things I did not do regularly until I was old enough to grasp that life is a short ride between worlds and that our highest calling along the way is to love one another. My father taught me these things. He learned them from our dogs.

Hunting Hurts

The problem with safety-rigging that first cup of coffee in the death-camp glow of a 7-Eleven when you're racing daylight to the deer woods is that you have not yet had any coffee. Which means you are unfit to supervise the operation. So it is only after a first sip, as I'm peeling out of the parking lot with a 24-ounce Styrofoam cup of scalding liquid between my legs, that I have the nagging sense that all is not well. I am aware only of the following impressions:

(1) Something seriously bad is about to happen.
(2) It's too late to do anything about it.
(3) I've been in this situation before.
(4) I'm in it again.

Then I recall that the click consummating the marriage of plastic lid and foam cup was a little off, a little hollow. Further, I remember that the pairing of cup and lid is an unforgiving system. Which is to say that the lid seals either perfectly or not at all. Which would seem to indicate that a large amount of hot liquid is likely to slosh backward onto my Sensitive Area in the near —

Suddenly I feel a blinding pain and the car grows loud with the sound of wailing and gnashing of teeth. I guide the vehicle onto the shoulder and commence extreme-pain avoidance measures that consist of pounding my head against the headrest, a welcome distraction from the more central affliction. Say what you will about the male reproductive machinery, it cannot be faulted for a lack of nerve endings.

It is several minutes before I regain my natural poise. I know that burns are best treated with a topical antibiotic and a loose, sterile bandage — neither of which I have. But a few drops of doe urine should discourage any germs from taking up residence in the affected area. And a brand-new scent wick loosely duct-taped over the wound will serve as a bandage. Back on the road and still suffering, I am nonetheless pleased. Mistakes are unavoidable in life. The great affair is to not let them distract you from your goal. I'm doing quite well in this respect. How many commercial wound treatments on the market also serve as deer attractants? I rest my case.

As I arrive at the woods, things are looking up on other fronts, too. I had been worried, for example, about finding my stand in the dark because I ran out of reflective trail markers the day before yesterday. (I meant to hang stands weeks ago. But my daughter Emma is bringing home first-grader homework now. Some nights it can take me a full hour to finish it. By then it's dark.) Sunlight has solved that problem. Approaching the streambed I'll follow to my stand, I startle five deer standing right out in the open not 40 yards away. They were doing that motionless brown trick of theirs that makes them invisible. Again, everything is going well. I had found abundant deer sign here two days ago. And my prediction that the animals would not seek new living quarters in the interim was right on the money.

Four hours later my patience on stand is rewarded. It's a party of four, all does. Unusually for midday, they are coming up the trail briskly. Stranger still, I see that they are following a smaller animal, a red fox, which trots along a few feet ahead as if leading them. It's the damnedest sight. They are 70 yards out when I have the presence of mind to rise and prepare to draw, forgetting the tuna sandwich in my lap, which tumbles 22 feet to the ground. Again, strangely, they do not take alarm but continue on.

Perhaps they are all fleeing the same threat, a dog. But they aren't looking back, and I heard no dog. Could it be that deer and the lower carnivores have put aside their ancient enmity as a first step in their plan to overthrow the common enemy, humans? I finally remember to draw, unsure whether my initial goal of putting a deer in the freezer has not been superseded by the need to stop a planetwide insurrection. This possibility is made moot, however, when at full draw my arrow amiably bounces off the drop-away rest and lodges between it and the bow.

Meanwhile, the deer, now aware of my efforts, have stopped right under my stand and are looking up at me. So is the fox. Using the forefinger of my bow hand, I try to flick the arrow up and back onto the fork. Since I have cut my arrows to a precise length, my finger's point of contact is the Bacon Skinner blade of a Rocket Ultimate Steel 100-grain broadhead. Aptly named, the blade is sharp enough that its cutting action doesn't even hurt. I try twice to flick my arrow back onto the rest, sustaining two wounds in the same place. By now, the fox has had enough. He skedaddles. The deer snort and follow. I let down the bow and the arrow clatters through the tree branches and plants itself in the leaves below. My finger bleeds copiously, my blood thinned by the single baby aspirin recommended for most middle-aged men.

Back in the car, bleeding, burned, and deerless, I tend to my wounds: a little more doe urine, another scent wick duct-taped to the affected area. And I'll be back tomorrow for sure. Success is just a matter of time for a determined guy with a positive outlook.

Morons Among Us

Ever wonder why so many folks have a less-than-flattering image of hunters? Let me explain it to you: There be morons among us. What's worse, the rest of us generally tolerate them. So if the antis ever succeed in banning hunting, it will be thanks to our generous support. We don't send them money, of course. But make no mistake: We contribute to their cause.

Imagine yourself a newly minted strategist working for an anti-hunting group. Within half an hour of starting your job, you'd be rubbing your hands with glee and telling your superiors, "These guys are a dream come true. We don't even have to think up ways to portray them as Neanderthals who are just after the thrill of the kill. They're already doing that for us!"

Visit enough hunting chat rooms and you'll see how. I found one in which a hunter was complaining that the buck he'd shot had died before he could taunt it with a dance he'd choreographed specially for the occasion. "I'm really into sports," the guy wrote. "I based my dance on some of Terrell Owens's moves after he scores a touchdown. It's this really in-your-face, I-own-you sort of deal. I worked pretty hard on all the moves, and I thought it would be cool for it to be the last thing some deer saw, knowing that I'd beaten it. I've done it for my friends at a bar, and they all thought it was hilarious. I'm hoping next year I get to do it for real." As sportsmen, I'm sure we can all share his frustration at a game animal that has the nerve to expire before a guy gets his chance to humiliate it. And it sure would be nice to meet his buddies.

On another site, a bowhunter wrote that he had always wanted to take a deer with a brain shot through the ear and that he had been waiting for just the right opportunity. His patience paid off, and everyone in the chat room was treated to a photo of what looked to be a yearling doe with a shaft angling out of the right side of her head. Forget that such a tiny target makes this an ethically indefensible shot. Forget that it shows no respect for the life of the animal. Forget — if you can — the grisly image itself, which brings to mind Saddam's torture-loving sons. No, the important thing here is that this hunter's wish to kill in a novel and satisfying (for him, at least) way was fulfilled.

There are unethical slobs in any sport, of course. And it's unfair to tar a whole group because of a few bad apples. But in both cases, these posts were met by a resounding absence of anger or censure. In fact, some who responded were admiring, even sympathetic.

Am I missing something? Are we hunters now convinced that the only thing that matters in the debate over our sport is numbers — so much so that we welcome anybody who hunts, no matter how twisted, into our ranks?

I hesitate to saddle up my high horse here, yet this stuff both scares and sickens me. We would do well to remember a few facts: Hunters are a minority in this country. There are a lot of people who want to abolish hunting. There are probably even more who are still forming opinions on the matter. The future of hunting depends on the actions of hunters and nonhunters alike. If we don't police the morons and slobs ourselves, we invite outsiders to step in and do it. I'm guilty myself. I was so distressed by what I saw online that I just walked away from my computer at the time.

Politics aside, there is something about crude behavior in a hunter that is not just offensive; it also eats at the soul of any true outdoorsman. These guys are cheapening something we love, something sacred. The longer I hunt, the more humbling I find the experience. Each time I walk into the woods with my bow, I rediscover how infinite nature is and how transitory and small I am. My carefully maintained suburban identity falls away like a dry husk. I become more alert. My consciousness opens up. I am focused, aware, alive. I am hunting.

Everything around me comes alive, too: the earth beneath my feet, the water in a brook, every leaf on every tree. The slightest tremor in the air is like the blast of a trumpet; the squawk of a distant woodpecker, a siren. Each step cracks open a new world. I am seeking an animal whose knowledge of this place is greater than mine will ever be. I come in humility precisely because no one is watching me, because I alone must live with the consequences of my actions here. Should I be granted a killing shot on a buck, I will kill. This is a confirmation of the hunt, the thing that makes being here so elemental and important. What I love beyond all reckoning, beyond my ability to explain even to myself, is this feeling of being more intensely alive than I've ever been.

As for the next moron hunter I bump into, fair warning: The gloves are off.

TAKE THAT, DEER

I started this deer season with the usual optimism, wondering if Milo Hanson and I could save on expenses by traveling the sport-show circuit together after I bagged my record buck. I did take a doe early on, which was encouraging. I mean, add 100 pounds and 220 inches of antlers and you've got yourself a retirement plan. But after a while I wondered if I weren't just another gullible steer on the ramp to the slaughterhouse. *Hey, must be some big fun going on in there or we wouldn't all be bunched up so tight to get in, right?*

I kept at it. By mid-October, I had year-and-a-half-old bucks running under my stand regularly. But at that time of year a young buck is about as horny and clueless as an eighth-grade boy, and I wasn't after the seed stock. Especially not when, at first light from 30 feet up a tulip poplar one November morning, I spotted something brown in the briers with antlers well outside its ears. The sight was so fleeting and the buck's silence in that crackly brush so unnerving that two minutes later I was no longer sure I'd actually seen it.

On another morning in trees so thick I ran out of shooting lanes as soon as I started climbing, I threw together a ground blind upwind of a trail that led into a deep, narrow slit of a stream valley. I had stolen my mom's new outdoor watercolor seat — a lightweight three-legged folder — for this purpose. (Mom is not even 80 yet and quite spry, so I knew she'd manage.) After a while, I threw out some doe bleats. Usually my bleats have the slightly hysterical edge of a sheep being molested in a dark parking garage, but this time I immediately heard something crunching my way. I saw 4 points on one side as he closed in, and I clipped onto my bowstring. Then my rangefinder bumped against the bow and the crunching stopped. It was a standoff, an agony of waiting. I shut my eyes and focused on the inside of my eyelids, on the red-and-black formlessness there that reminds you the utility bills are due. I made myself breathe in through the nose for four counts, hold for four, exhale for four. I remembered — I have no idea why — being punished at summer camp 40 years ago for mouthing off to a counselor. I'd been made to stand outside the bunkhouse after lights-out with a brick in both outstretched arms while the mosquitoes formed a buffet line along me.

Then the buck took another crunching step my way. Shifting ever so slightly to draw, I felt the stool going over backward. I went along for the ride. That afternoon I brusquely returned it to the woman who'd brought me into the world. Thanks for nothing, Mom.

Next, having drawn an archery tag for Kansas, I invited myself to hunt the property of Richard Stucky, a farmer I'd pheasant hunted with once. I knew he'd be too polite to refuse. To my surprise I felt no qualms as he and his son, Steve, busted their humps to put me on the biggest buck I'd ever hunted. He was an 8-pointer headed toward 10, with tines that kept going long after you'd gotten the message, much like the poorer sort of revival speaker. With a rifle, I could have killed that sucker three times over four days. I thought I had him the first morning, 12 feet up in a creekbottom hedge apple, when I heard that telltale steady crunch. Trembling, I drew as the sound grew louder. One step more and . . . the luckiest possum on earth waddled into view.

An hour later, the buck showed along the far edge of the bottom, just out of range and shielded by brush. I grunted. He stopped, looked my way, and bedded down. He stared in my direction for 20 minutes before standing, relieving himself, and walking on.

That afternoon, Richard and Steve staged an elaborate push based on where they guessed the deer would be bedded. Steve approached on horseback to lessen the spook factor; Richard flanked him at a slow walk. Half an hour later the buck passed within 45 yards of where they'd posted me, walking but not scared, once again screened.

On the fourth day, I saw a bobcat and heard a chorus of squirrels barking at it like PTA moms who have just discovered a registered sex offender in the neighborhood. Then, at last light, I heard two deer walking. The final smudge of sunset sky was turning gray and purple at the edges. Five minutes later they came out into the open. It was past legal light, but through my binoculars I could make out the buck with a doe, both standing broadside at 30 yards, relaxed and feeding. Those long, curving tines glowed radioactively in the amplified light.

I'd done my best and come up short. He'd

beaten me fair and square. When that happens, all you can do is take one last look through the glasses and grope for the words to salute your quarry. "You son of a bitch," I said.

MR. NOVEMBER

It was November, the great hinge on which the deer hunter's year swings, and the only thing that mattered was being in the woods. I was driving on expired plates and taking my meals standing at convenience-store microwaves while my gas pumped outside. It didn't seem right that my dinner cost $2.19 while my car's was $35, but until they make a vehicle that runs on beef-and-bean burritos, there's not much I can do about it.

The wide-racked buck that had ghosted through the briers and into my dreams at the end of October paid me another visit on November 6. Inching up a yellow poplar that morning, I had been thinking that another 6 feet would be about right — good lanes and high enough to avoid detection — when a tug on my 30-foot tote rope stopped me short. That's how gone I was, thinking 36 feet was a reasonable height. I had barely settled in when he came along, scent-checking for estrous does. I grunted. He kept walking. Louder. Seventy yards off, he froze, looked for the challenger at the base of my tree, let his eyes travel up. With three effortless arcs, he vanished into cover. I still hadn't registered points, just that he was bigger than anything I'd ever seen in these woods.

Nine days later, dusk overtook me in a tree downwind of what I fervently hoped was what biologists call a staging area. Suddenly, a doe scampered into the clearing and began feeding. The buck crashed through the bushes, grunting nonstop, not 5 feet behind her. All I remember is that she was drawing him away, that it looked like 30 yards, and that it took forever to find a lane and the spot behind his shoulder. Then he was running downhill as previously nonexistent does exploded like popcorn out of the brush. I had a fleeting memory of the shot feeling good. Then my mental odometer turned up all goose eggs. I did have the sense to climb down slowly, but I couldn't have told you where he'd been, whether he'd been moving, or if my arrow had hit him. Nor could I find any part of the arrow, blood, or the divot he would have made on his first leap. I stood there, figuring that either I'd just shot at a huge deer or it was time for a psychiatric intervention. I needed to find out which.

My friend Jay Wheeler and his son Joe, hunting nearby, came over when they saw me walking in circles. Joe found blood 40 yards past where I was looking. We followed the trail, one of us standing at the last drop while the other two looked ahead. There would be a big medallion of red, then nothing for 10 yards, then a pinprick of blood. In an hour we pushed the trail just 40 yards using my penlight. Then Joe went for a bigger flashlight and a rechargeable lantern, but at 6 p.m. he and his father had to leave. I blood-trailed alone for another hour, going an additional 30 yards before the flashlight died. I left the lantern glowing faintly at the last spot and raced to a store for batteries. Three hours later, I had gotten only another 150 yards. I would not allow myself to wonder if I'd killed him. My universe had telescoped down to the square foot of ground before me, to the text of leaves and dirt I was kneeling to examine. I hadn't eaten in 10 hours, but I wasn't hungry. I was feeding on light, leaves, and pinpricks of blood. At 10 p.m. the second set of batteries ran down. I backtracked to the creek for a reference point, whereupon I discovered it was now running uphill. I knew these woods, knew it was impossible to get truly lost. But the wave of panic that coursed through me knew things, too. I bushwhacked toward the faint glow of a distant road, stopping for neither bush nor brier nor my own hat being snagged off my head.

The storm that moved in that night was worse than predicted and lasted for 24 hours. It wasn't until the day after that I could get back into the woods. And then, at 8:30 on a sun-washed morning, I walked right to him, antlers bright against the dark ground. He was 104 steps from where I'd left the lantern, 20 inches wide, an 8-pointer with bases I could just encircle with my thumb and forefinger, the right brow tine broken halfway up. I'd taken out one lung but nicked the other. The only record book he'd make was the one that mattered: mine. I had taken the boss dog in this patch of woods. I stroked his flank, at last loosing the euphoria, relief, and sadness that floods over you when a long-held dream is granted.

I took the next day off, rested, even opened some bills. The following day, sitting at my desk, I realized it was still November and therefore a good time to hunt. I shut my computer down and threw my gear in the car. Machines can always be turned back on. But November is a show that closes after 30 days no matter how good the reviews. The next one won't come along for 11 months, and tickets to it are not guaranteed. I'd get around to the bills and the license plates. Right after November.

ACKNOWLEDGMENTS

I am indebted to many people who helped move this book from the theoretical plane to the actual one. I would like first to thank my parents. Without them, there's no telling where I might be right now.

I'd like to thank everyone at *Field & Stream:* Sid Evans, the magazine's editor, urged me to do this book. A wise reader and editor with great instincts for the story, he often believes in me when others do not, including me. Jean McKenna, who edits the monthly column I currently write, keeps me on schedule, and listens to me whine when I can't think up anything to say. David E. Petzal, beneath whose gruff exterior lies an even more blunt and bearish second layer. Whether there's anything beyond that is known but to God. Mike Toth and Anthony Licata, both of whom continue to give me work in spite of the jokes I subject them to over the telephone. Slaton White, who first let me into the pages of the magazine.

Finally, I'd like to thank my former wife, Jane Ashley. Maybe we aren't meant to be married to one another, but nobody can say we didn't try, and I still love you.

ABOUT THE AUTHOR

Bill Heavey is an editor at large for *Field & Stream,* which he has written for since 1993. His work has appeared in numerous publications including *Men's Journal, Outside, The Washington Post,* the *Los Angeles Times,* and *The Best American Magazine Writing.*

The employees of Thorndike Press hope you have enjoyed this Large Print book. All our Thorndike and Wheeler Large Print titles are designed for easy reading, and all our books are made to last. Other Thorndike Press Large Print books are available at your library, through selected bookstores, or directly from us.

For information about titles, please call:
(800) 223-1244

or visit our Web site at:
http://gale.cengage.com/thorndike

To share your comments, please write:
Publisher
Thorndike Press
295 Kennedy Memorial Drive
Waterville, ME 04901